During

Oppression

People

Evolve & with growth

Everyone

Rises

Above

Written By: Stanley Cox

D.O.P.E. E.R.A.   Stanley Cox

<u>10 Keys to Being Dope</u>

- Keeping a Positive Perspective
- Staying Dope
- Giving Roses
- Pushing Peace
- Being Your Own Biggest Fan
- Respecting Others' Happiness
- Fathers Over Figures
- Giving Back
- Reinvent the Role Models
- Resilience, Accountability & Responsibility

D.O.P.E. E.R.A.   Stanley Cox

This Book is Dedicated to:

My Mommy, Daddy & Libby

D.O.P.E. E.R.A.   Stanley Cox

Forward

My name is Derrick D. Grace II and I'd like to extend my gratitude for even being considered to carry out this task, for such a solid individual.

Let me start by reminding and reassuring the person reading this article of melanated history, that this man is more than necessary for the culture. Very few have crossed so many dimensions and worlds, yet still stayed true to self and their people. From his independent grind, influence like his classic about Twitter, to street intelligence spewing all over ESPN, his love for the people, his attentiveness to Fatherhood, and much more. Very few escape the ego that destroys so many of us in the streets, to not only do such but double back and empower others to do the same... through Example that is! Fab is more than motivation, Fab is a walking testament to every word he speaks. The energy of an 80's hustler, the heart and support of our people in the 90's, and the relativity to still be influencing both the young and old generation in 2018. I'm positive this reading will be nothing more than a priceless and timeless piece of work in regard to our morals, ambition, and a code of ethics that so badly need to be restored. I ask one favor of anyone reading this book, ask yourself what's value to you and what are you doing to preserve and extend it? I ask that to say this, I've watched our era die to be the know it all in Black History class but happily sleep on and forget to celebrate the living,

D.O.P.E. E.R.A.   Stanley Cox

current, and future history. Fab has been that is that, and most likely will remain that. Pedestal his existence while he can appreciate it. Those same videos we repost and see so often on social media and say damn! That elder person was so far ahead of their time during their hay day, genuine, and needed... We can use him right now, we need him now, if only he was here to fix this... Will one day be Fab. He's been a stand-up man, gem, and rarity for multiple generations of people. Enjoy this reading, his type only comes around every 15 years. Fab has treated me like family since the day we spoke, extended his space to my family, and kept us fitted in Dope Era on every visit.

If you appreciate me, how can you not appreciate him and his efforts to restore the feeling we yearn for as a generation and people. Dope Era or No Era!

D.O.P.E. E.R.A.   Stanley Cox

Introduction

I was about 9 years old when I received a letter from my father (Who was in the federal penitentiary) that said, "out of all my kids, you are the chosen one" ... I saved that letter. I probably still have it somewhere buried in boxes of things. Some good some rubbish, my Father would always tell me "you are special"

Pick something you wanna do in life and apply yourself and I promise you'll be successful. I don't have many memories of him, I can count on my hands the ones I do. But I vividly remember his love, his smile and the passion he had towards me being something. I often think if he was still here how different would things have turned out. Oh well, like Momma use to "it is what is". I was born January 23rd 198, my parents Stanley Petey Cox Sr. & Desire Anita Jefferey, my Dad had a few kids, but I was my Momma's only child ... born and raised in the "CITY OF DOPE", Oakland California

I faced obstacle after obstacle but now when I look in the mirror I can honestly say I am proud of the man I've become....

Thinking back on my childhood years I smile because even though we were barely getting by my mother keep me laced.... she nearly gave her life to raise me right. I mean I had everything a kid/teenager could want, video game systems, clothes, all the fly Shoes (in the hood the only ones that mattered were Jordan's) and I had every pair. They called me a

D.O.P.E. E.R.A.   Stanley Cox

spoiled kid, but they had no idea that behind this image of a
spoil child was a story many of them couldn't understand.

I was about 7 years old, me and my Mom

We're staying on 59th and telegraph (Top of Bushrod Park)
and I had a "MR. T" piggy bank.

My mom's friend J.D gave me 100 dollars (man I thought I was
rich) I put it in my bank, went to sleep dreaming of all the
things I was going to do when I woke up with this money, only
to wake up to a nightmare. I checked my bank and it was gone.
I ran into the room to tell my Momma my money was missing
and soon as I saw her, there she was HIGH as Bobby and
Whitney at A Hollywood coke party. She was sitting on the
edge of the bed and Man I lost it........ I began screaming, yelling,
cussing and fussing, because I knew she took my money and
bought crack with it. MY HEART BROKE .. I was so
frustrated, I was crying and shaking uncontrollably. It wasn't
just the money y'all, it was the fact she was still getting high and
she lied to me...

It's crazy how a 7-year-old could recognize things like that, but
that was the times "the Dope Era". Seeing me like that broke
her down literally like that was the shortest high she ever had.

I got dressed and demanded she take me to my granny's house.
In that moment I hated her and never wanted to see her again..
(man, what I would do just to see her now) ......

D.O.P.E. E.R.A.   Stanley Cox

I packed a small bag and she dropped me off at my granny house and she said next time you see me I'll be clean, and my life will be together, and I'll never let you down ever again!!!!!!!! She kissed me on forehead gave me a big hug, told me Good and she'll be back soon...Fast-forward to the pick-up....

When she came and got me she was so beautiful & healthy smiling from ear to ear and from that day she never used Crack again, she made a promise to Me that anything I wanted in life she would work hard for me to get. hence for the reason she worked 3 jobs, so I could have the title "spoiled kid" .. but none of the kids in the neighborhood knew we was a paycheck away from an eviction note every month ... Hahahaha I can laugh now but it was serious, the struggle was real.

I wouldn't be who I am today if it wasn't for my mother that woman's will to push me to be something was beyond belief, she supported everything I did 100%

Basketball games, baseball games, football, shows, assembly's you name it she was there in the front row screaming that's my baby

My biggest fan, for real for real. She instilled in me a confidence that can't be described.

When they ask me where do I get my drive from I always revert back to my Momma

Because no matter the hurdle, obstacle or challenge she always found a way to get over it.

D.O.P.E. E.R.A.   Stanley Cox

She Taught me the art of figuring it out

So much game I received from both of my parents though, that's why I dedicate this book to them.

I grew up in the Dope Era

A time in American history that some would love to forget, some could never forget, and others wish they were there to see what the fuss was about. Street hustlers flooded every corner, and young ghetto children sacrificed their dreams for fortunes. At the same time zeros turned into hero's and on the flip side heroes turned into zero's. It was the chances you took.

Diving head first into this street life.

Prom queens became Dope fiends

And athletic jocks became knocks

It was what it was ... THE DOPE ERA ...

We learned to work we what we had because of most of us didn't have much.

We became creative, Street Pharmacist conjured up poison serving it to the lab rats, who just so happen to be our Mothers and Fathers, Aunties, Uncles, Sisters and Brothers.

Creating zombie's real life, night of the living dead... but every coin has another side

The money these dudes was making

D.O.P.E. E.R.A.   Stanley Cox

Was motivation to the poor

Gave a hope in the unseen.

My approach was a lil different than all of my friends though.

I never wanted to sell drugs because I saw how it destroyed my family, it took me away from my mother and it took my father away from earth. So, my plan was to be Dope without DOPE!!!!!

I began writing around 93-94 (I still have the Rap Books to prove it) haha...I was 11 years old in my room playing sonic the hedgehog and my Mother walked in with a look I'll never forget she said, "pause the game let me talk to you". I responded, "yes Momma" .. she said "your daddy was shot last night" my heart dropped...... I instantly started crying I said "is he ok" she said "yes but it's something else" I'm like hell what could be worse than that.... she says he's been diagnosed AS BEING H.I.V positive ..... Man, I ain't know what to say at this time only person I know who had AIDS was EAZY & MAGIC JOHNSON..... I thoroughly had no clue of what it was, I was broken, I mean badly I didn't wanna talk to nobody, I was filled up with anger & hurt, I was lost!!!!!!!

I picked up a pen and just started jotting down my life story in the form of poems.

Daddy died in 94 I was 12

D.O.P.E. E.R.A.   Stanley Cox

Momma had met this man named Robert Jamerison. Good dude, didn't smoke, didn't drink was a pure class act cat all around guy

They hit it off real cool ended up getting married.

I remember we drove to Reno

That was the happiest and prettiest I saw mommy that day in an all-white dress

Just a smiling, she overcame so much in her life that moment was magical

BLACK CINDERELLA..

I'll never forget my Stepbrother was on his Nubian Hype, this foo had on an A's short fit with a Nappy High Top

That's Marty for you... over the years Him and Dez became inseparable. She helped grow him into a man by providing a solid woman's shoulder and heart he could rely on.

We threw the word step out the window years ago that's my BROTHER!! And ASIA J that's my sister... crazy how much her & Libby look alike It's almost scary...

I wanted to thank Rob my Step-Dad for stepping up and taking me in like his own.

I love Him to this day for all the lessons he showed, he grew up in the streets in and out of jail as a young kid so when it came to

D.O.P.E. E.R.A.   Stanley Cox

Love he had it just didn't know how to express it or show it that much. But I know in his heart he loved me unconditionally. He taught me how to drive, how to get up and go work for what you want and how to be a man of principle and responsibility. I LOVE YOU POPS.......

My Momma only messed with Players, Hustlers or Ex- Pimps, that just was her thing.

She couldn't fuck with no soft cat, he couldn't handle her .. she talked back and didn't listen lol..,

Her last dude she had until her last breath will always have a place in my heart because thru thick n thin, in sickness & health he never let her side.. Cedric Harrison aka P.C (Prince Charming) player for real jack!!!

That's my dog and I got nothing but love for this cat. Old country boy up outta that DALLAS Texas. Bonfire to the Left suited and booted Gee'd up from the feet up type player,

Loved him some Dez and she loved him help me a lot in the maturation of my adult game. Always giving me pointers and vital tips to churn from a boy to man in this game as the old school say lacing my boots and kept my game sharp. That on top of the fact he never left my momma when she was sick

He got lifetime gold card with me love you P!!

Play on player!!!

D.O.P.E. E.R.A.   Stanley Cox

I was 28 when my mother died, my daughter was 2. If it wasn't for Liberty I can't honestly say I'd still be here. Not in a million years could I have seen my Super Woman checking out the game so early, I always thought me and her would grow old together. She used to always joke and say, "nigga u Bet not put me in no damn retirement home, Ima QUEEN I deserve a castle". You did, Momma and yes that was my queen

I often cry myself to sleep at night wishing I could hear her voice, tell her about all the things going on in my life, brag to her about my accomplishments meanwhile hearing her brag to her friends about mine

That was my best friend in the whole world and I miss her dearly...

And if this place that people always Talk about really exist I know she's in heaven looking down on me.. smiling saying That's my baby!!!!!!

This one for you Momma!!!

I wrote this book to inspire, motivate, and encourage people to challenge themselves

Set goals, go after their dreams, never be discouraged by failure, never stop ascending,

Keep trucking, laugh at hatred, face your fears, stand on truth, refuse to except no's, stay focused, dream big, Love, Live, explore, adventure and most of all Be proud of yourself.

D.O.P.E. E.R.A.   Stanley Cox

In the end it will be ok and if it's not ok

Then it's not the end.....

Spread love it's the Oakland way

Baby BABY!!!!!!!

THE ERA

D.O.P.E. E.R.A.   Stanley Cox

Key One:
Keeping a Positive Perspective

Message: Love, Happiness & Relationships

People bring old baggage to a new vacation spot.

Your next shouldn't have to suffer from inflictions

caused by your ex

#StartOver

Drain the poison before you start the next

relationship.

Message: Game

There's nothing wrong with complimenting someone

or allowing them to know that you appreciate their

existence. Some say that they don't give people props

D.O.P.E. E.R.A.   Stanley Cox

because people acting

"Hollywood".

Let me tell you something. If a person does, in fact,

act a certain way that's an insult to their character,

not yours.

It just shows how they were raised.

Message: Positivity & Encouragement

Never fight negativity with negativity.

Nothing comes from that. Don't nobody got time to

be bitter all the damn time!!!!!

My Era was Dope.It was about Loving and Living,

not Hating and Killing.

Get money and spread blessings!

D.O.P.E. E.R.A.   Stanley Cox

Message: Goals, Hustle & Ambition

Turn your passions into your profession.

Grind for it, don't whine for it. Dreams do come true.

It's all up to you! Spread love! Go for it. You can do it.

There's no such thing as impossible; the proof is in

the word itself IM possible. Go get it.

Message: Positivity & Encouragement

Never allow someone else's character to bring your

own into question...REMAIN YOU

Keep the codes, morals, rules, and regulations that

you were raised with intact.

D.O.P.E. E.R.A.   Stanley Cox

KEEP IT G, even when others switch the alphabet.

Message: Game

Mistakes build character.

It's ok to mess up, if you learn from the experience.

I've been going through a lot, but it has positioned

me to present my best to the world.

Message: Positivity & Encouragement

Keep going further, people.

Never allow the world to minimize your perspective.

Keep dreaming and look at the bigger picture.

Never get complacent.

Dream on baby!

D.O.P.E. E.R.A.   Stanley Cox

Message: Love, Happiness & Relationships

I refuse to be the victim of someone else's lack of
understanding.

If we can't agree to disagree, then let us agree to part
ways.

I am too old for the "let me just say something" type
or the "let me get the last word" type.

I've overcome too many obstacles in my life to let
another person feel the pleasure of pushing me off my
square.

We regularly stay in situations that put our peace in
jeopardy.

Let me say this loud and clear, never let love force
you to LOSE.

D.O.P.E. E.R.A.   Stanley Cox

Don't lose yourself, lose your mind, lose your morals,

lose your heart, or LOSE YOUR PEACE.

Say it with me: MY PEACE BELONGS TO ME!!!!!

It's mine.

BLOCK ALL VIOLATORS.

Message: Positivity & Encouragement

Let's keep a positive perspective.

One must understand that we're living in a world of

negativity today.

Everyone wants to disrupt someone else's positivity

As I sit back and look at my life I realize all the things

that I've done that may not have been considered

positive. This just goes to show that some of us need

D.O.P.E. E.R.A.   Stanley Cox

negativity to recognize the difference between good

and bad.

I never frown down upon the things that I've done

because they make me who I am.

They give me character.

When you embrace what is considered to be a flaw

by others, you'll realize that it's actually a gem.

Perspective allows us the ability to know the

difference between a gem and a hard rock.

I've realized it's not always what you're looking at,

but how you see.

D.O.P.E. E.R.A.   Stanley Cox

Message: Positivity & Encouragement

A person is truly emancipated when they have freed themselves of all skepticism and criticism.

They're ok with the opinion of others because it actually does not reflect on them directly.

Some people die for respect but live for nothing.

I think the demise of a man is when he allows his ego to be bigger than who he actually is.

I am not defined by my ego, nor am I defined by my possessions.

There a lot of people in this world who are defined by their positions and that's the only way they identify.

But what happens if your possessions are taken away? Then, who are you?

D.O.P.E. E.R.A.   Stanley Cox

Message: Positivity & Encouragement

Life is a game of chess.

I was told to never play chess with a stranger, especially if it is for free because the whole time you're just playing a game they're processing your patterns. You really must understand the concept of it.

Life is all about patterns and although you may feel like someone can't read you. Patterns never lie.

Be careful who you have allowed to learn your patterns.

Betrayal can't come from outside. It always must come from within your inner circle.

How can you be betrayed by a complete stranger?

D.O.P.E. E.R.A.   Stanley Cox

You have to know someone to be betrayed by them. Always watch everyone and just when they think they know your patterns, switch it up on them.

Message: Positivity & Encouragement

I used to be afraid to lose until I learned that even in my losses there are lessons.

Those lessons can be turned into victories because it's a victory to learn from your losses.

I didn't lose if I learned something.

Message: Positivity & Encouragement

There's a thin line between a perfectionist and a procrastinator. Someone will say "I'm just waiting for

D.O.P.E. E.R.A.   Stanley Cox

the right moment." but then they're still waiting 10

years later for that right time to come.

Perfectionists don't even really realize that they're

actually procrastinators.

Why put something off that can be done today?

Why wait for tomorrow?

Tomorrow is not promised, so I'd say handle it today.

Message: Positivity & Encouragement

Opportunity is right around the corner and the sad

thing is that many people never leave the block to

search for it.

D.O.P.E. E.R.A.   Stanley Cox

Message: Positivity &Encouragement

I lost my father at the age of 12. Being young and not
having a father was an experience that I wasn't alone
in experiencing because all my friends never had
their fathers either.

It was a blessing to even have had a father for 12
years.

Although my dad wasn't the most positive, he was a
great man, he was very smart, very intellectual, and
very loving.

I wish I could have had a little bit more time with
him but losing him early was another thing that has
shaped my character.

D.O.P.E. E.R.A.   Stanley Cox

It taught me that there will be adversity in life, but the true character of a man is how he responds to adversity.

Message: Positivity & Encouragement

I've lost several times in my life and what has stuck out to me the most is my ability to own up to my losses.

There was a time where I would make a million excuses, but I never want to get to a point where would I speak down to the community that raised me.

I am living, learning and sharing my wisdom and knowledge as I get it in order to prepare my people for better days.

D.O.P.E. E.R.A.   Stanley Cox

Message: Haterz

People's perception of you will always be dependent
on their perspectives. I refuse to accept ridicule from
someone whose bias is strictly based on ulterior
motives.

One thing I know is that I'm happy and blessed and
give all I get to the masses in my messages and my
movement.

Thank you.

Message: Haterz

Make the blessings count, don't just count your
blessings.

D.O.P.E. E.R.A.   Stanley Cox

Life is about getting through. It's not about
complaining about what you are going through.
PAIN IS LOVE.

Message: Game

They say that numbers don't lie but I'll tell you this,
they also don't tell the full story.
We are living in a time where people will do
anything to bolster their numbers.
Niggas buy followers and use cheat codes for stats.
Man, you ain't going to do anything but to fool the
fools. Slow and steady. That's how I was taught to
play the game. Make in-game adjustments to get
better as the game goes on. In the end, I am going to
play longer, and my stats will be reflected based on

D.O.P.E. E.R.A.   Stanley Cox

facts. No, I ain't got to cheat you to beat you. Now that I can be proud of.

Message: Positivity & Encouragement

We have to get to the days of educating each other,

teaching and learning from one another.

Take a second to ask yourself, does the person you

interact and engage with the most teach you

anything? Have you taught them anything?

Is there a person you are mad at right now? Is there a

conversation that can be had to clear things up? If so,

then maybe you should have it.

Life is too short to hold grudges against those you

love. Now if it's a fuck nigga (fuck em) but you get

my point!!! I think it's time to heal one another.

Let's help instead of hurt.

D.O.P.E. E.R.A.   Stanley Cox

Build instead of bullshit.

#DopeEraPhilosophy.

Message: Game

You'd better get yourself something to do.

Foolish pride will get you fried!

Take care of yourself and handle your

responsibilities, but first be responsible for

something! Remember, it can get better.

GET YOU A PROGRAM.

Message: Game

Let's grade ourselves using a progress report.

You can lie to everyone in the world, but when you

lie to yourself, you destroy yourself.

D.O.P.E. E.R.A.   Stanley Cox

How can you love someone else more than you love yourself? Have you stopped ascending? Are you complacent? Are you happy? Is this enough? Are you ok with just being ok? Questions show interest. How much interest have you invested in yourself? We all have room for improvement. Let's continue to grow and ascend.

Message: Love, Happiness & Relationships
If a person doesn't love themselves, then there is no possibility of them doing anything more than lusting after you. I don't even wanna be with someone who loves me more than they love themselves. Stay focused, stay driven and stay accomplishing goals.

D.O.P.E. E.R.A.   Stanley Cox

It's not about how long you live. It's about what you

can accomplish during your time here.

You can get almost anything back in life but don't

waste your time trying to be perfect.

Just stay productive.

I enjoy my imperfections because they fit me

perfectly and they make me perfectly imperfect.

Message: Positivity & Encouragement

READ THE CAPTION!!!!!!

Don't make these liars and scammers have you feeling

bad for not having the courage to take penitentiary

chances just to flex.

They're out here robbing people and living life foul

just to be in style.

D.O.P.E. E.R.A.   Stanley Cox

Well if the facade requires me to compromise my
integrity, my inner peace and my karma points just to
fit in, Imma stand outside and keep playing my game.
Now I'm not telling you not to enjoy life and I'm not
telling you not to live a little, but what I am saying is
don't feel bad if you're not able to do so yet.
Notice how I said YET. Map out a plan.
Let me tell you this "all-star flexing" gonna set a lot of
people back some months just for some fake stunts
and likes. It ain't worth it. Besides, you ain't miss
nothing. It's just a bunch of people on they're phones.
Blah blah blah. It's all flex talk.
Live life but always go at your own speed.
Pace yourself. Don't erase yourself.

D.O.P.E. E.R.A.   Stanley Cox

Message: Positivity & Encouragement

Don't let the pressures of social media affect your real

life. A lot of people just know how to make it look

good. The message of the today is: don't believe the

flex.

The grass is greener on the other side because that

shit is FAKE! (And chemically treated.)

Stay in your own lane, remain true to yourself, and

trust your struggle.

Message: Positivity & Encouragement

You can't expect something good to happen to you if

there is no good in you.

You have to remain resilient and focused on the game

plan. Everybody at the game is not there to cheer for

you. I know it hurts when you're playing a home

D.O.P.E. E.R.A.   Stanley Cox

game and you see an individual rooting for the other

side, but hey it happens. Stick to the game plan.

Focus on WINNING.

If you can't pull a win off at least improve and play

better than your last game.

More examples. Fewer excuses!!

Keep working!!!!

Message: Game

The ways of the world are turning us into mutes and

mimes.

We have to bring back the dinner table

conversations and meetings of the masses and invite

dialogue because at this rate there will be no more

human experiences

We have to do better!!!!

D.O.P.E. E.R.A.   Stanley Cox

Key Two:

Staying Dope

Message: Game

You don't need to be the face that everyone knows to

make a living and have a career.

I'll always pick money over fame.

Let em think you fell off. You know that you're well

off.

Message: Game

Being rich doesn't make you real & being broke

doesn't make you fake.

D.O.P.E. E.R.A.   Stanley Cox

The principles of life you identify with reflect in your

character.

If all you have is money and fame, then you're pretty

much possession less.

Message: Game

Stop switching lanes just to keep up with

commuters.

Go at your own speed.

Stay in your own lane.

You'll get there.

You set the speed limit.

Don't crash trying to please others.

D.O.P.E. E.R.A.   Stanley Cox

Message: Game

We have to begin to seek beauty in all creations. Be

proud of something today that has nothing to do

with monetary status.

Smile and enjoy the essence of life, stress-free.

Message: Goals, Hustle & Ambition

In life, there are two kinds of people you will come

across, builders and destroyers. Builders seek and

search for the opportunity to create. Destroyers focus

on the dream to the point where it distracts them

from the dream.

I've never been blinded by the allure of the material.

I'm driven by dreams.

I get lost in my vision, but I never lose the vision.

D.O.P.E. E.R.A.   Stanley Cox

Message: Positivity & Encouragement

Don't be quick to judge others because they sin

differently.

Learn and teach, spread love and peace.

The key to enjoying life is establishing an

understanding.

Message: Positivity & Encouragement

You have to be comfortable with being

uncomfortable.

Stare adversity in the face, look fear in the eye, and

fight for what you believe in!

Stay focused and dream hard, but make your reality

that much more lit.

#DopeEraDuty

D.O.P.E. E.R.A.   Stanley Cox

Message: Haterz

You have to cocoon as a human from a boy to man,

from darkness to light.

Go from not knowing to understanding.

Growing past people's understanding of you is what

causes friction and hatred. And because of this, some

individuals want to leave you behind and never see

you morph from a caterpillar to a butterfly.

But keep growing, keep living and no matter what,

keep shining baby!

Message: Game

Getting rid of poison cultivates pureness.

I am trying my best every day to turn my words into

wisdom and manifest inner peace.

D.O.P.E. E.R.A.   Stanley Cox

A pure love, a pure happiness, a pure prosperous

perspective.

It's a challenge but challenges alongside chances

create champions. I am born to be a winner.

Message: Love, Happiness & Relationships

One thing I know is: you better love yourself.

Tell yourself that you are proud of you.

Message: Positivity & Encouragement

GET ON YOUR GRIND.

Nobody has to support you.

Nobody owes you anything.

It says a lot about you if you let hating stop your

progress.

If it's meant to be, you will get there.

D.O.P.E. E.R.A.   Stanley Cox

KEEP GRINDING! STOP WHINING!

Message: Game

Let's get back to loving, protecting, communicating

and valuing US...

We are broken people with great reason.

It's up to US to help build each other back up.

Message: Game

My Mother used to tell me, "Life is a jungle, Stan.

Realize the nature of the beast you are dealing with.

Don't be naïve, Stan, everyone that smiles in your face

ain't your friend.

Be mindful, Stan, there are animals in this jungle that

are starving, and their hunger pains may lead to them

wanting to feast on you.

D.O.P.E. E.R.A.   Stanley Cox

Pay attention, Stan, watch your surroundings, being

smart is not being scared. Don't let your pride get you

fried.

Stay woke, Stan, don't sleep on these creatures out

here.

It's ok to swim in the shadows."

I just wish certain things weren't the way they are,

but who am I to think that I can change the ways of

the wild.

I can only hope to teach my brothers and sisters

tactics of survival.

I take full responsibility for the happenings on my

watch, however, when I am not around I know shit

be an open plain for animals to play.

D.O.P.E. E.R.A.   Stanley Cox

I pray for understanding and I hope to instill my

sentiments in my folks to create a more peaceful

environment.

One must be held accountable for one's actions and

reactions.

When shit went wrong for me, I used to search for

someone to blame.

Now I blame myself for putting myself for not being

better prepared.

And I always hear my Mother's voice in my head,

"Remember the rules of the jungle."

P.S. Time is the biggest snitch of all, it will bring to

light all that was done in the dark.

#DopeEraPhilosophy.

Message: Game

D.O.P.E. E.R.A.   Stanley Cox

When you entertain a clown, not only did you buy a
ticket, you become a part of the circus.

Message: Game

You will learn so much about the players in it, which

will teach you about the players around you. The

only thing that changes are the names.

The positions stay the same.

Pawns, rooks, bishops, knights, kings, and queens.

Message: Game

Truth always comes with a witness.

When you are doing something right, the stars will

give you confirmation and if you are paying attention

you will receive signs.

You gotta get up, get out and get something.

D.O.P.E. E.R.A.   Stanley Cox

If you get better, it can get better.

#DopeEraPerspective.

Message: Goals, Hustle & Ambition

Stay on course people!!!

Dedicate yourself to your grind!!

There are no shortcuts, no side-streets.

Respect the road.

It doesn't matter what time you get there. It's just

about getting there!

My momma always told me, "The slow grind is better

than no grind. Give it a second and you'll be there in

no time."

Message: Positivity & Encouragement

Stand on your truths.

D.O.P.E. E.R.A.   Stanley Cox

Dispose of the lies.

Dedicate yourself to your plans.

No matter how tempting it may be to stray away,

stay focused on your path and what is meant for you

down the road, shall appear.

Receive the blessings, don't run from them...

Love and light.

Message: Game

Know your "no" and "know". For so-called

successful people, learning how to say no has proven

to be one of the most difficult things. There's a thin

line between slighting people and hurting yourself.

Know enough to know you don't know it all, but you

know enough to know what's right for you. Don't

throw away a royal flush cause you fell for the bluff....

D.O.P.E. E.R.A.   Stanley Cox

Change the way you look at things and the things

you look at will change.

Message: Positivity & Encouragement

You have to do the best you can to stay on the right

side of right.

There is no right way to do the wrong thing.

Message: Positivity & Encouragement

Your infrastructure has a lot to do with your forward

progress and how long you with progress!!!

Don't be afraid to seek help.

D.O.P.E. E.R.A.   Stanley Cox

Message: Game

Put some value on yourself and stop risking all you've

worked for people who don't work for nothing.

Earn your stripes.

Earn your respect.

Earn your loyalty.

Earn your rewards.

GRIND FOR IT, DON'T WHINE FOR IT.

Message: Game

Be blessed, grateful, and thankful.

Always stand for something and on something!!

All the money in the world can't buy you peace of

mind and happiness. I'm happy and remain positive

through it all because I mind my business and know

who I am. I am living my dreams.

D.O.P.E. E.R.A.   Stanley Cox

This was all a dream!!!

Message: Game

My daddy used to say, "life's not about hopes and

dreams, it's about ways and means."

How will you make the things you dream about your

Reality???

Plan for it.

We have all heard the saying "if you fail to plan, you

plan to fail".

That has never failed me.

All I'm doing from now on is planning the takeover.

#DopeEraDynasty

D.O.P.E. E.R.A.   Stanley Cox

Message: Game

What is success to you?

What ensures your happiness and what lengths are

you willing to travel to secure it?

When your poor money seems like it's the only

remedy for your problems

When you get a little money, you realize BIGGIE

WASN'T LYING.

More money, more problems.

I used to pray for all the things I have now, and the

crazy part is my material gains are what I am least

happy about.

I'm prouder of the man I've become, the father I've

become, the growth in my perspective, the

knowledge I've received and the intelligence that has

D.O.P.E. E.R.A.   Stanley Cox

come with that, and the wisdom that I'm able to

share.

I'm happy about the way I'm learning to treat people

because it's actually a reflection of how I treat myself

I went from a dream chaser to an event planner.

I am awaiting new adventures in my life.

I am sticking to the script, staying on course of the

plan and showing others in the process that progress

is attainable just remain focused!!

That's success to me!

D.O.P.E. E.R.A.   Stanley Cox

Key Three:

Giving Roses

Message: Goals, Hustle, & Ambition

Don't be too proud to ask for help or be over
emotional when people don't respond how you
expect them to.

KEEP ASKING.

THE ANSWER WILL ONLY BE A YES OR A NO.

Remain persistent until you get a definitive answer!!!

D.O.P.E. E.R.A.   Stanley Cox

Message: Game

I remember when "I GOT YOU" actually meant you had someone. Niggas (especially industry niggas) ruined the meaning!!! #FACTS Don't trip, I GOT ME!

Never put your fate in somebody else's hands!!!! ALWAYS PREPARE TO HAVE YOURSELF.

Respect the real ones who still value their word.

Message: Goals, Hustle, & Ambition

Don't get too caught up in the temperature.

D.O.P.E. E.R.A.   Stanley Cox

People get HOT & think that it's gonna be forever
and when they cool off nobody fucks with them
anymore.

Nobody stays hot forever baby!!!

Don't let the buzz make you forget that one day you
still have to cross paths with those that you acted
funny with!!!

Message: Game

Ignore the hate. Adore the love. You are a reflection
of what you give.

You're entertaining energy too!!!

D.O.P.E. E.R.A.   Stanley Cox

Sometimes we focus so much on who's hating that we actually overlook the ones right under our nose that are overflowing with love!

BE GREAT TODAY.

Message: Positivity & Encouragement

When people do things for you, be appreciative and grateful. Do not feel entitled like they owe you.

I am thankful for anyone who has done anything for me. To any one that has donated to any event, has come to any show or has shown love and support in any form or fashion, I JUST WANT TO SAY, THANK YOU!!!!!

D.O.P.E. E.R.A.   Stanley Cox

Message: Goals, Hustle & Ambition

Don't be so consumed with the boss lifestyle that you

forget to be humble to a grinder's dreams or a

creator's vision

HUMILITY. Make it work.

Message: Positivity & Encouragement

Life is about growing and building

It's not about being bitter!!!!

These two guys did a lot for me in my career and I'm

thankful that I'm around to tell them thank

you!!!! @bigvon @djmindmotion THE GUYS!

D.O.P.E. E.R.A.   Stanley Cox

Message: Positivity & Encouragement

It's a beautiful day!!!! Love the journey.

Enjoy the adventure. Be thankful for adversity.
Appreciate the obstacles. Respect the course. Always
do your best and NEVER EVER GIVE UP.

Message: Positivity & Encouragement

A wise warrior uses all things the that are designed
to hurt him as ammunition to help him.

You know you never know how strong you are until
strength is the only thing you can rely on. When my
Mother died, it was the worst day of my life. I

D.O.P.E. E.R.A.   Stanley Cox

struggled and contemplated giving up but quickly

realized that would be a total slap in the face to her

parenting.

I was taught that no matter how bad it gets, we don't

quit. A player doesn't keep score, we just keep up.

Always be conscious that yesterday's score has

nothing to do with game.

Keep pushing no matter what game is on. Be the

phoenix that rises from the ashes of doubt and

abandonment.

Don't worry about the people that count you out, as

long as you never count yourself out, you

will always be accounted for.

D.O.P.E. E.R.A.   Stanley Cox

Message: Positivity & Encouragement

Spreading love is far better than plaguing the world
with hatred, spite, negative energy and bad vibes.

A good vibe can put you in a head space you never
knew existed.

Positivity changes your perception of everything bad.

Seek beauty in all creations instead of highlighting
negativity.

A person would critique and ignore everything
positive about you for the one wrong thing they

wish to promote.

Don't leave out the good in all the bad news you're
sharing.

D.O.P.E. E.R.A.   Stanley Cox

Message: Game

As Tupac Amaru Shakur said:

It's time to HEAL EACH OTHER.

BE REAL WITH EACH OTHER!!!!

Let's build and teach, help and listen.

As a people, we need to open our eyes.

Instead of complaints, let's cultivate solutions. What are you doing to create change????

Don't let the money change you, create change with the money.

#DopeEraPerspective.

D.O.P.E. E.R.A.   Stanley Cox

Message: Positivity & Encouragement

The hardest thing for people to do nowadays is give

credit where credit is due. Unfortunately, the reason

is because everybody's in competition with

everybody.

Me, I never really worried about what somebody else

is eating as long as I know that my plate

was cool.

Even if it wasn't full at least I put something in my

stomach.

I know people nowadays always plate watching.

That's what I like to call them. They used to be called

pocket watchers.

D.O.P.E. E.R.A.   Stanley Cox

My grandmother used to say what they eat don't make you shit.

I used to laugh but didn't really understand what she meant until I got older.

What I realized is that their digestive system is totally different than mine and although their plate may look good, it doesn't always mean it's seasoned right. From that point on I realized that I wasn't worried about what nobody else was eating.

I'm only focused on how I will make my meals.

D.O.P.E. E.R.A.   Stanley Cox

Message: Positivity & Encouragement

Some people are so competitive that they refuse to give compliments. My parents were players. My Daddy was like the coolest dude on earth.

He looked like Billy Dee Williams fresh out of a movie and he always brought great energy around when I saw him.

No matter what he did in his off time or in his private time, he always kept a clean-cut look. When I was young I didn't even know that he used drugs because he was always so fresh and always smelled so good. Whenever he saw another player in the game, he always recognized him and greeted him with godly gestures.

D.O.P.E. E.R.A.   Stanley Cox

There was no hate in him. He saw another man that was clean and fly and he said, hey player. I see you, baby.

I made a mental note of that. Whenever I recognize a player in the game, I always give him roses.

I always tell a man that he's looking good or smelling good. I make a person feel good.

Like my uncle Keith Smith said, "a player is going to keep another player with the game because you know how the game goes and you want to see a good player always playing."

But there's not too many real players anymore.

It seems like this generation is having an identity crisis because social media has actually made us

D.O.P.E. E.R.A.   Stanley Cox

antisocial people that don't communicate with each other.

Rarely do you see people conversing about things that have value or substance, and when they see someone who really has confidence and great aura they become intimidated.

That intimidation leads to hatred, more denial, never giving flowers to those that deserve it.

I was at the barbershop the other day and I heard these kids talking and one said, "Yeah, dude be clean, but I never tell him now because he's already confident enough. He don't need to hear that from me."

D.O.P.E. E.R.A.   Stanley Cox

In my mind I was like wow, is that how people

think? They don't want to give somebody credit

because they're confident?

When you're sure about yourself, you really don't

have to worry about what others think.

I know I don't, I'm ok with being "BOOTSY" aka

different.

My Uncle Foonie told me people in our city call cats

bootsy because they don't understand their

difference.

He then followed up and said being bootsy will

always separate you from the rest of the pack.

Embrace your difference.

D.O.P.E. E.R.A.   Stanley Cox

Then, it's no big deal when you recognize someone

doing the same exact thing and you can share vibes

with them

If you ever complimented someone and they fronted

on you or shined you on,

Aye man, that's not on you that's on them. That

character flaw sticks to that person.

Message: Positivity & Encouragement

Support is worth more than money.

Sometimes a person just needs a shoulder to lean on

or someone to vent to.

D.O.P.E. E.R.A.   Stanley Cox

They need someone to call in the middle of the night and share with knowing that they will protect the information and keep it sacred.

It's been a long time coming and there's so much more to come but if it all ended today I can say this guy is my friend.

I want to extend a Happy Birthday to him.

Keep shining, keep growing, and keep being you my CRAZY ASS AQUARIUS BROTHER!!!!!!!!!!!!!!!!!

@philthyrichfod

D.O.P.E. E.R.A.   Stanley Cox

Message: Game

Everybody's intentions are not the same.

When a person reveals who they are, believe them.

We're not collaborating. We're not letting off the

gas. Everything will be accounted for.

Message: Positivity & Encouragement

We must be mindful about creating clarity but at

what cost does clarity come?

One of my mentors @zoetharoasta told me "We can't

diss someone in public and apologize in private." So,

you must utilize the same platforms that you used to

bring the situation to the surface, to remove it.

D.O.P.E. E.R.A.   Stanley Cox

But here is where the game comes in. We were raised in the ghettos and streets and there is a code and unwritten obligation that we must still uphold.

Both a pro and a con of social media nowadays is its accessibility to people from all walks of life.

Here you have a worldwide forum that gives everyone a microphone to project whatever they choose to spew.

Gangstas, Killers, Thugs, Pimps, Prostitutes, Vagabonds, Lawyers, Doctors and Squares,

imagine explaining some super exclusives street details to someone who has never step foot on the curb.

They won't understand it.

D.O.P.E. E.R.A.   Stanley Cox

In this age of enlightenment, you must understand

that your perspective may not be fully grasped.

Message: Positivity & Encouragement

Love and light.

Remember it can get better

And if it does, throw the ladders down when you get

up. Help build the bridge of understanding, so we

can all over stand.

Because what's understood doesn't have to be

explained. Dope Era philosophy.

Message: Positivity & Encouragement

D.O.P.E. E.R.A.   Stanley Cox

We have to stop being blind to a broken man's
dream.

We have to stop being dismissive of others inability
to live this "ballers life".

I'm not telling you not to enjoy your life or feel guilty
because you are living in good favor. Never be
ashamed of your accomplishments or feel like you
have to diminish your light because others aren't
shining...nah this little light of mine, I'm gonna let it
shine.

Just be mindful that even the richest man in the
world will still face problems, still has adversity, still
goes through losses, still experiences death, sickness
and darkness.

D.O.P.E. E.R.A.   Stanley Cox

Those who have risen from the pits of poverty should

hold themselves to an unwritten obligation to at

least attempt to help lift others up!!!

If you reach the top and have a chance to build

ladders, throw some back down. Remember it's up to

us to make this world better!!!

DOPE ERA PHILOSOPHY!

Message: Love, Happiness & Relationships

True happiness is shown in how you treat others.

You can't truly be happy for anyone else until you've

emotionally and mentally emancipated for yourself.

We have to check our issues inside of ourselves.

D.O.P.E. E.R.A.   Stanley Cox

Cleanse your body of hateful parasites and watch

how happiness begins to flow into your life.

#DopeEraPerspective.

Message: Positivity & Encouragement

STOP BEING AFRAID TO DELIVER ROSES!

IT'S NOT DICK RIDING WHEN YOU'RE

SHOWING LOVE!!!!!!

If a nigga acts funny when you're giving him props,

that's not on you. It's on them. Don't stop showing

love.

I wanna see you win even if I'm not responsible for

your victory.

D.O.P.E. E.R.A.   Stanley Cox

I just love the game. I love to see Cats play and be
rewarded for their hard work!!!! This tough guy shit
really got us fucked up. It's turned us into haters, for
real!!!

Spread love. I bet you you'll be way more happier and
can sleep easier at night!!

Message: Positivity & Encouragement

When you grow up with someone sometimes you
want things to be like they were when you were kids.

But responsibilities kick in and the wind blows us in
different directions in life. My life has been like Peter
Pan.

D.O.P.E. E.R.A.   Stanley Cox

I never wanna grow out of my imagination and I often dream of this world where my friends can see things the same way.

After venting and "sub-gramming" one of my best friends we jumped on the phone with each other and talked about the ways that our lives are different now.

We can't just do the same things we used to do

But, the friendship never changed. We just had to learn to adjust and bust moves more accurately. In my mind I just want the old gang to hang forever and I was being selfish, I guess.

That's Stanley for you.

D.O.P.E. E.R.A.   Stanley Cox

But after having this phone conversation with one of my childhood Best Friends/Brother/Cousin I was humbled and appreciative.

He walked into the Dope Era store opening night and it brought the biggest smile to my face. I just wanna say thank you @isthatrio for that lesson!!!

OAKANDA FOREVER

Message: Positivity & Encouragement

At the end of the day, projecting positivity is what all it's about.

It's about sharing and shedding light even in your darkest moments and knowing that sun comes after the rain.

D.O.P.E. E.R.A.   Stanley Cox

Be somebody's light today.

You never know how much shade has clouded their potential for positivity. In the end it will be ok and if it's not ok, then it's not the end.

D.O.P.E. E.R.A.   Stanley Cox

Key Four:

Pushing Peace

Message: Haterz

Never let the insecurities of others determine your

happiness.

Message: Game

When spend your time trying to please others, you

cheat yourself out of precious moments.

Don't let the lack of responsibility of others make

you feel compelled to attach their stress to your back!

D.O.P.E. E.R.A.   Stanley Cox

Carry your own weight.

Stay focused.

And make sure you are happy.

Message: Positivity & Encouragement

Don't spend your todays weeping over the
yesterdays, for tomorrow might never come.

But if it does, have a fresh attitude and be thankful
for the opportunity to make it better.

D.O.P.E. E.R.A.   Stanley Cox

Message: Game

We have to learn to treat another's home as we

would want ours treated.

Respect respects Respect.

I only want the best for me and mine.

And I will always represent the REAL.

You must stand on principle when you a man in

position.

Message: Game

The Game doesn't always go the way we planned it,

but I knew what it was when I signed up.

D.O.P.E. E.R.A.   Stanley Cox

So, I take the bitter with the streets.

It's just the way of the street.

Message: Game

Stop vouching for Sucka Shit. We're allowing people
with no credible credentials to uphold the standards
and codes in this world. We're adhering to the
bullshit they put into the universe with no facts or
proof, all because they said it first. We gotta do
better.

D.O.P.E. E.R.A.   Stanley Cox

Message: Positivity & Encouragement

We have to stop contributing to the humiliation of

our people for our selfish entertainment.

We have to be better with the handling of each other

as a people.

Let's grow up!

Message: Positivity & Encouragement

It doesn't hurt to help.

Erase the hatred and selfishness from your heart and

watch more blessings flow in for you!

D.O.P.E. E.R.A.   Stanley Cox

Message: Game

Stop judging people based on the life you knew they once lived.

And those who have changed, stop judging people who are still in that world.

In order for us to grow, we must be inspired by those who are living proof that change is possible.

We can help and heal, not hurt and hamper.

Message: Positivity & Encouragement

Be there for the healing, not the headlines.

D.O.P.E. E.R.A.   Stanley Cox

Message: Positivity & Encouragement

NEGATIVITY IS NOT THE WAY.

It only destroys us!!!!

Whose down to build????????????!????!!!

Let's push positive movements.

Message: Positivity & Encouragement

One Block, One Thug, One Hood with One Love.

You are what you entertain.

There's a lot of circus acts going around recruiting

clowns.

Be careful what you sign up for....

D.O.P.E. E.R.A.   Stanley Cox

Message: Positivity & Encouragement

It is pivotal that we create the media we wish to share with the world.

People will not only pray for your downfall, but they will film your downfall.

It's time we focused on building and healing.

I'm here for the HEALING, NOT THE HEADLINES!!!

Take a minute and ask yourself what positive thing have you done today?

Let's replenish our community's ecosystems with clean news and positive action.

D.O.P.E. E.R.A.   Stanley Cox

N.B.R.M. (New Black Role Models).

Message: Game

In this era Sucka shit is now the cool thing. Let's start with the DISRESPECT! Since when is it ok to curse in front of your parents or elders? In my day my granny was not going for that. Nowadays, even the giants suffer from the "Little man complex".

Our kings argue with pawns of the world, as the pawns stick out their chests hoping to sway the decision of the king.

You have to grow through your potential and excel in your position through work.

D.O.P.E. E.R.A.   Stanley Cox

You wanna be a Gangsta? Open a business in your community that creates employment and opportunity.

That's what the real O. G's did back in my day. That's who I aspired to be like. Change starts with the self.

Who's willing to do the work though????? WE NEED EACH OTHER.

You gonna build shit or bullshit?

Message: Game

My granny used to say, "When they don't respect your presence, make then miss you with your absence...."

D.O.P.E. E.R.A.   Stanley Cox

A player can be confused for a weak man, but one must always remember:

A smart man can play stupid, but a stupid man can never play smart.

The truth is in the detail.

My love for my Hood, Block, and Brothers goes beyond life.

I want for my Brothers as I want for myself but sometimes I don't think that the reciprocity is there.

Ask any of my friends, I've never left them stranded and would go to the end of the earth to protect them.

Unfortunately, people don't check on the strong because they always feel like we are good, or we will be ok.

D.O.P.E. E.R.A.   Stanley Cox

I could never say I'm free if my people are still

mentally enslaved.

It's time we break the chains.

Message: Positivity & Encouragement

Be thankful that you can experience emotion, good or

bad. There're many graves all over the world that are

void of emotion.

Message: Positivity & Encouragement

Don't let image define you.

You are who you are with or without possessions

D.O.P.E. E.R.A.   Stanley Cox

If you aren't then all you are those possessions.

At the end of the day, I am just Stanley still figuring myself out.

WHO ARE YOU?

Message: Positivity & Encouragement

WAKE UP AND APPLY YOURSELF.

Have you ever seen a squirrel stop trying to get a nut???

Go to work every day.

Dig down and search for your inner greatness and cultivate it every chance you get.

Be ready, your time will come, but don't confuse eagerness for readiness.

D.O.P.E. E.R.A.   Stanley Cox

You can't swim in the ocean if you just learned to
swim.

Man look, those currents are different.

Get right and when it's time you will know.

#DopeEraPhilosophy.

Message: Game

I love my people (all people) but especially those
who share the same pigmentation as me. I often
wish that I could save everyone because I'm a
dreamer.

But, I am smart enough to know that I am not smart
at all.

I seek counsel from other intellects, peers, colleagues,
and mentors. The purpose of my search is to embody

D.O.P.E. E.R.A.   Stanley Cox

methods of mashing up all the information and

serving it to the ones who need it the most.

You can't feed a baby steak. They will choke on it.

You must mash their food.

That's what has to happen to knowledge and

wisdom. We must not forget who we are trying to

feed...the babies.

Be blessed people today.

#DopeEraPhilosophy

Message: Positivity & Encouragement

Protect Your People

Work For You or They Will Work You

Show Up and Show Out

D.O.P.E. E.R.A.   Stanley Cox

Always Be Ready

Grind for it, don't whine for it!

#DopeEraDuties

Message: Positivity & Encouragement

It's never YOURS...just YOUR TURN.

When it doesn't work out or go in their favor, they'll
always go back to who they're comfortable with.

Enjoy the times, but most of all stay focused.

Know your worth, baby!

There are 8 billion people in the world, but there's
only 1 you.

D.O.P.E. E.R.A.   Stanley Cox

Never get too comfortable

You never know who they're really working for.

Biggie asked who shot ya????

I ask, "who sent you????"

Message: Game

The truth doesn't travel as far as the lies do, but the
Truth does REMAIN.

Some would rather be real temporarily and receive
the false praise for a moment.

Then there are others like me who'd rather forever
remain solid.

When I'm long gone, my authenticity will forever be
young!!!

D.O.P.E. E.R.A.   Stanley Cox

Message: Game

You have to "REVEAL TO HEAL". I put my all into
this album "Thug Tears".

It wasn't about a check for me it was about Checking
me!!!!

It was about looking in the mirror and being real.

Stop running around with a robot's tendencies.

Don't act like you don't feel nothing like you don't
hurt like you're not going through something

It was about being open, allowing the world access
to my journal and helping others come to the
realization that they may need some help.

The power is in the people and politics they address.

D.O.P.E. E.R.A.   Stanley Cox

I'm saying all this to say:

Don't get caught up in the numbers just remain

REAL TO UNVEILING YOUR TRUTHS.

Being 100 % honest helps you sleep better at night!!!

Dope era or no era.

Be the Big Homie you wish you had

Message: Game

In the world of unjust judges, we must learn to settle

out of court.

Understand that most of the people that criticize and

critique you have never worked for anything. So, they

D.O.P.E. E.R.A.   Stanley Cox

could never imagine the gratitude one feels when being rewarded something.

Let me tell you this: don't let nobody make you feel bad for what you do with your hard-earned money.

Truthfully it ain't they damn business anyway!!!

Utilize yours wisely.

I respect it!!!

Message: Game

What are your motivations? Who are your Influences? What do you believe in? Who do you aspire to be like?

Ask yourself these questions.

D.O.P.E. E.R.A.   Stanley Cox

If you don't come up with a solid answer or if you
keep drawing blanks, let's start filling them in. Let's
begin to be the changes we wish to see.

It must start with those that we paint as role models
and leaders.

No one is perfect. Allow for a few mistakes.

Let's keep building.

Message: Positivity & Encouragement

As a people, we have been conditioned to go to
drastic lengths to be accepted. We are so used to
wearing a mask, that we have forgotten who we truly
are.

D.O.P.E. E.R.A.   Stanley Cox

I knew a lady who wore contacts for so long that she put that her eyes were the color of her contacts on her driver's license.

We've lied to ourselves and have been so ashamed of our flaws that we've hidden them so long that we've forgotten that they were there.

That repression is what drives us into deeper states of depression, drug abuse, alcoholism, and financial immaturity.

All this to try to prove something to the others.

D.O.P.E. E.R.A.   Stanley Cox

Message: Positivity & Encouragement

Why is it that the majority of times a black person is slandered, it is their own people throwing the stones?

In the words of Tupac: "I really feel like it's time to heal each other and be real with each other.

We are experiencing a race of babies that hate the ladies and actually hate each other.

We are failing to communicate, forcing the hands of violence and destruction upon our own.

We must do better.

Victims are victimizing innocent subjects because hurt people hurt people."

D.O.P.E. E.R.A.   Stanley Cox

Message: Positivity & Encouragement

PROTECT THE PROTECTERS OF OUR

CULTURE.

Illuminate the light of those who Shine a little

brighter.

The right STARS and the chosen people will always

put light on everyone else

Message: Positivity & Encouragement

Tell somebody you love them today

Spread love.

It's the OAKLAND WAY!!!

D.O.P.E. E.R.A.   Stanley Cox

Message: Positivity & Encouragement

We have to do a better job protecting our legacies,

our presence, and our purpose.

We must provide our people with all the support:

moral support, spiritual support and most

importantly, financial support.

Start Praying for your people and stop PREYING on

your people.

D.O.P.E. E.R.A.   Stanley Cox

Key Five:
Being Your Own
Biggest Fan

Message: Positivity & Encouragement

There's nothing wrong with being proud of your accomplishments but like I always say remember that what is given can be taken away, so never get so high on your accomplishments that you are blind to the sober reality of others. Tupac once said, "never be blind to a broken man's dream."

Message: Goals, Hustle & Ambition

Sometimes you just have to get up and go!!!! Your dreams are not just gon fall in your lap.

D.O.P.E. E.R.A.   Stanley Cox

It may not come to the city you're in.

GO TO IT!!! REAL LIFE MEETING!!!!

If you're chasing dreams, get up and go, baby!!!!

Message: Game

Be strong enough to let go and patient enough to

wait for what you deserve.

Settling is a form of slavery.

Some jewels never lose their shine!!

Message: Game

The secret to walking on water is: never let the

onlookers see the rocks aligned right beneath the

water.

Never reveal all your tricks and tips.

D.O.P.E. E.R.A.   Stanley Cox

Message: Goals, Hustle & Ambition

Don't limit your effort to views!!!

Sooner or later they will all go back and review what

they overlooked!!

Stay Working!!!

Message: Goals, Hustle & Ambition

Here are a few Keys to Success:

#1. Keep Pushing Your Brand

#2. Stay Dropping Heat (And Fuck Whoever

Doesn't Like It)

#3. Never Stop Believing in Yourself

#4. Stay Consistent, Stay Working, and Always

Network

#5. Listen to Older People. Period.

D.O.P.E. E.R.A.   Stanley Cox

Message: Goals, Hustle & Ambition

There have been special people who have aided my

journey and supported me along this expedition, but

ambition, motivation, and drive can go a long way!!!

If you believe then you can achieve!

Just look at me.

Message: Goals, Hustle & Ambition

Don't whine for it, grind for it.

Invest focus and time for it.

I'm on a date with destiny driving down the road of

dreams.

I'm not stopping or slowing down for anybody trying

to get me to waste gas.

Focus.

D.O.P.E. E.R.A.   Stanley Cox

Message to the dreamers: turn your dreams into

doings.

Message: Goals, Hustle & Ambition

Don't stop going after your dreams.

Don't lose the vision.

I know what it's like to be poor.

I don't know what it's like being rich.

Message: Positivity & Encouragement

Live in your creations.

Don't lose your dream.

Get lost in your dreams.

Message: Game

Start working on your own dreams now or you will

work on someone else's forever.

D.O.P.E. E.R.A.   Stanley Cox

Message: Positivity & Encouragement

Inspire to be better.

Don't get bitter, get better

Don't get mad, get motivated.

Don't get pissed off, get ya paper on!!!

Message: Game

I don't knock anything anyone does.

I ENJOY THE PROCESS OF MY PROGRESS!!!!

Message: Goals, Hustle & Ambition

A dream chaser has to have tunnel vision.

See only the dream and then live it.

D.O.P.E. E.R.A.   Stanley Cox

Message: Goals, Hustle & Ambition

The worst thing you can do is give a half-assed approach to your dreams and goals. The effort you put in will be reciprocated back by the universe. I've never seen somebody who dedicates themselves 100%, sacrifices, starves their distractions, practices, and works hard not be a receiver of the universe's réparations.

Message: Game

Don't worry about letting someone else down.

Just focus on keeping yourself up.

Confidence is confirmation.

BE HUMBLE BUT STILL HIGHLY FOND OF YOURSELF

D.O.P.E. E.R.A.   Stanley Cox

Message: Goals, Hustle & Ambition

Let your imagination be bigger than your reality and

your reality will eventually seem like a fairytale.

Message: Game

Grow into your potential and get it with like-minded

individuals.

Message: Goals, Hustle & Ambition

Never let your audience determine your ambition.

Go as hard no matter if its 1 person or 1 million

people.

No days off!

D.O.P.E. E.R.A.   Stanley Cox

Message: Goals, Hustle & Ambition

It's going to take some time but enjoy your journey

because the more bricks you lay, the more solid the

foundation.

Message: Positivity & Encouragement

If your style of play is working for you and yours,

don't change your game, make others adjust to you.

I can't worry about nobody's numbers, only mine.

I'm happy with my humble.

Message: Positivity & Encouragement

Unfortunately, selfish is the new trend. We're so

selfish nowadays we don't even speak anymore. We

don't talk about building. We don't talk about fixing

or creating solutions. We all independently complain

D.O.P.E. E.R.A.   Stanley Cox

about our problems. I say OUR problems because
it's our worldly problems that have been created, so
it's up to us to iron them out!!!!
In life, you BUILD SHIT, or you BULLSHIT.

Message: Game

One thing I refuse to do is give up on me. Drive has to
outweigh complacency in order to move forward.
Look in the mirror and say, I didn't come this far to
come this far. Keep going and don't quit on you!

Message: Game

Vulnerability and love have been stripped from our
emotions making us incapable of being human.
Everyone is living this façade claiming to be real but
in actuality, they're the total opposite.

D.O.P.E. E.R.A.   Stanley Cox

Message: Game

Create legs for your dreams so they can walk on

their own.

Ain't nothing change but the numbers on the

calendar.

It's hard to carry on when no one loves you but keep

pushing and believing in your destination.

Know that you are going to get there no matter how

tough or crowded the road is.

Message: Positivity & Encouragement

I'd rather be self-less than selfish! Blaming others

won't change your position. Self-accountability is

pivotal in the forward trajectory of one's positive

elevation.

D.O.P.E. E.R.A.   Stanley Cox

Message: Positivity & Encouragement

THE WORLD NEEDS MORE LOVE.

And as a people, we need each other.

Would you kill the world to save yourself?

When asked this question as a child, I said "yes."

My mentor replied, "Then you would have the

greatest war story in the history of the world and no

one to share it with."

Message: Haterz

They will lie about you, spit on you and accuse you of

all kinds of wrongdoings. They will call you a thief, a

bigot, and a hypocrite all while they themselves are

guilty of the very accusations they are throwing your

way. And when they see their true self, they don't

have the strength and they claim you should have to

D.O.P.E. E.R.A.   Stanley Cox

deal with their struggles. MISTAKES HAPPEN, IT'S

OK. I've already been through the worst.

DOPE ERA OR NO ERA.

WE NOT STOPPING.

Message: Game

DO WHAT WORKS FOR YOU!!!

STAND ON YOUR OWN PLAN!!!!

Message: Love, Happiness & Relationships

Pick one thing that you're proud of, that you're

excited about, something that rings your bell, that

melts your heart, that tickles your fancy and SMILE

LIKE YOUR WINNING NUMBER WAS CALLED!!!

CHEESE!!!!!!

Push love.

D.O.P.E. E.R.A.   Stanley Cox

The world needs more of it.

Message: Haterz

Stop being someone's burden and focus on how you

can become someone's blessing.

If you can't bring nothing to the table, at least be the

first to wash the dishes when dinner is done!

Message: Haterz

You're not broke if you spend your money on being a

responsible adult.

You're on that grown-up shit.

You're broke when you're piss poor morally and out

here trying to make your lows seem high!

Who you flexing for???

D.O.P.E. E.R.A.   Stanley Cox

Message: Goals, Hustle & Ambition

The lack of support should be all the support you

need because it forces you to show yourself what

you're made of.

Message: Game

You going to be a buyer or seller?????

If you chose seller then the number 1 rule in the game

is to keep something for sale.

Keep grinding.

Keep hustling.

Keep your product available.

And no matter what, stay firm on what you want.

D.O.P.E. E.R.A.   Stanley Cox

Message: Haterz

Stop giving up on you.

Stop giving the haters all that satisfaction.

You gon let these doubters impose their will on you?

When they tell you that you ain't nothing you believe

them?

Look in the mirror right now and tell yourself:

"No matter who fucks with me, I fuck with me! And I

refuse to give up on me!"

Message: Game

Do good and receive good. It might not come back

instantly but trust on this, it will come. Our energy

will be a reflection of our works with the universe.

D.O.P.E. E.R.A.   Stanley Cox

Message: Game

Sometimes it takes years and years for that overnight

sensation to be born!

Focus and know that.

Message: Game

Allow gradual growth when dealing with

transformations and transitions. Common sense ain't

common and some learn at a different pace. Slow

down and build with your Brothers and Sisters and

stop getting frustrated because they aren't picking it

up as fast as you received it.

Be blessed.

D.O.P.E. E.R.A.   Stanley Cox

Message: Game

Don't ever beg anybody for acceptance or inclusion.

Let your work be an example of why you should be

in it.

Feel like you're not getting noticed?

Work harder!!!!! (Or smarter.)

Message: Goals, Hustle & Ambition

When it's all said and done will you be the person

that blamed everyone else for your mishaps, misery,

and misfortune?

Or will you tell everyone, even Jesus, "I got the wheel.

Just guide me!" You have to take your destiny in your

hands and never let the fate of your legacy be

controlled by another.

#sundaysermons

D.O.P.E. E.R.A.   Stanley Cox

Key Six:

Respecting Others'

Happiness

Message: Love, Happiness & Relationships

Sometimes the best way is to walk away. Save the

heartbreak.

Message: Love, Happiness & Relationships

Shout out to all the lovers. Just because you're lonely,

heartbroken, bitter, spiteful, angry or jealous don't be

a grouch and deny someone their happiness today!

D.O.P.E. E.R.A.   Stanley Cox

HAPPY LOVE DAY!!!! Can't find someone to love or love you back? LOVE YOURSELF!

Message: Positivity Encouragement

There's nothing better than happiness. I HOPE ALL OF YOU REACH A HIGH LEVEL OF HAPPINESS IN YOUR LIFE. Try every day to reach that level and if you can't do it for yourself, try and make someone smile.

Message: Haterz

When you're on a winning streak you'll notice how jealous, envious, sneaky, and hateful the ones you call friends and family are.

That's why I Fuck with Em without Fucking with EM!!!!!!

D.O.P.E. E.R.A.   Stanley Cox

Watch the ones that are close and make sure they do
what they're supposed to do.

Message: Positivity & Encouragement

You ever had someone hit you and you ain't answer

for whatever reason, then they text you and say some

shit like, "I know you're up. I just saw you post..."

What?!?!

Are you really monitoring my page? Where they do

that at?

Ok so I posted something, that doesn't mean that I

feel like talking or texting. We all have our days

where we move at our own speed and there's

absolutely nothing wrong with that.

D.O.P.E. E.R.A.   Stanley Cox

There are some days where you are forehead deep in
work only to come up for air once the task is
accomplished.

Go ahead and get your busy on.

Go fill up your schedule, go get lost in your program.

At the end of the day, feel good about having

something to and never let anyone make you feel

different about handling your business!!!

RESPECT MY BUSY!!

Message: Positivity & Encouragement

Embrace new beginnings, especially if they're

positive.

Support your people who are transitioning as best

you can.

D.O.P.E. E.R.A.   Stanley Cox

You would be shocked at how far a little

encouragement can go.

Message: Game

Listen, the phrase: "I'm just saying," is hating!!

Stop being a damn critic unless you get paid to do

that, if not CLAP FOR A PERSON!!!

Be happy that a person is making themselves happy

doing what they're doing!!!!

Stop complaining, stop assuming, stop being messy

and noisy, stop wishing failure on people, stop

talking down about people and then upping yourself

in the same sentence.

NEGATIVITY IS WHACK!!

Love and light.

D.O.P.E. E.R.A.   Stanley Cox

Message: Game

STOP BEING AFRAID OF COMPETITION.

You are allowing your insecurities to get the best of

you!

Projecting your fears forms hatred in your mind and

fucks your thinking up!

We have to do better.

Remember it can get better if you work on it.

Message: Game

REMAIN PRICELESS, DON'T SELL OUT FOR

PENNIES!

Get up and get yourself in position.

Program your GPS towards the BAG!!!

D.O.P.E. E.R.A.   Stanley Cox

It's always a game, you just gotta remember what
position you play and understand that making others
better is the test of a true leader and STAR.
But you have to make sure you are ok first!

Message: Positivity & Encouragement
Peace of mind is established when sharing a piece of
mind. There are conversations that can iron out every
misunderstanding. Complications come when
people refuse to communicate.
Fault and responsibility dance to the same rhythm.
Some things may not be your fault, but you are still
responsible for them.
You wanna get the universe in your favor? Obey the
call of nature's dynamics.

D.O.P.E. E.R.A.   Stanley Cox

People sometimes wonder how I remain so positive

in the midst of chaotic and catastrophic negativity

and I say the same thing time after time.

Message: Positivity & Encouragement

I'm old enough to understand that some don't have

the understanding because some things can't be

understood from the angles people look at them.

If you change the way you look at things, the things

you look at begin to change.

I can only push this perspective on those who wish

to see light and I understand that dark minded

thinkers will have no interest in my vision.

I separate myself from anyone who wouldn't relight

my candle if they see it going out.

You have to surround yourself around the light.

D.O.P.E. E.R.A.   Stanley Cox

It's the only way to stay LIT!!! (AYE)

Message: Positivity & Encouragement

Know the nature of the beast you're dealing with and

never think for one second that you're completely

safe in the JUNGLE.

Even if you are looked at as a king.

Would you rather be the ☐ or the ☐?

When I was younger I wanted to be the lion.

As I get older, I have more aspirations to be like the

fox.

The fox is smart, a thinker, a planner, witty and

evasive.

D.O.P.E. E.R.A.   Stanley Cox

Message: Positivity & Encouragement

Every day might not be a good day, but you can find

something good in every day.

Message: Game

You have to wait your turn.

While you're waiting, be getting your game ready.

Get your mind right. Get your hustle on.

Study, research, work out, prepare, so when your

number is called,

You READY!!!!

Don't be so quick to win.

Don't run for class president just because you're

popular, if you're not ready to handle the

responsibilities that come with the position you're

running for.

D.O.P.E. E.R.A.   Stanley Cox

Be blessed. Be smart.

Message: Game

Know when you're the blessing you have to be the
bearer of other's burdens.

Message: Positivity & Encouragement

I find myself seeing the things in people no one else
can see. My visions make me go a little harder for
them. I've fought battles for individuals solely based
off hidden potential. I don't know if it was empathy
or sympathy, but I feel the need to take a little bit
more time with others.
I love my Brothers and Sisters, Friends and Family
passionately and I want the best for them. All I hope
is that they want the same for me.

D.O.P.E. E.R.A.   Stanley Cox

But, you can't want something for someone more

than they want it for themselves

We should focus on healing ourselves so that we can

be an example to our people that the healing process

is possible because LORD KNOWS WE NEED IT.

Message: Game

It's time we fix the leaks in our support systems.

Push mine like you'd push yours if you're really in

my corner!

Let me know that you're in my corner, not just in my

circle taking up space!

Message: Game

How enlightened can you be if you constantly throw

shade on others?

D.O.P.E. E.R.A.   Stanley Cox

If you are as enlightened as you proclaim to be, then someone's happiness should make you happy even if you're not responsible for it.

I don't care what you believe in, if you're happy and it gives you hope and positive affirmation, then I'm all for it.

Message: Game

Today you can resurrect yourself and rise from behind the shadow of the clouds that have been blocking your blessings.

Be the change that you wish to see!!

Smile, laugh, love and live.

D.O.P.E. E.R.A.   Stanley Cox

Message: Game

The cold thing about mental health in the hood or

the black community, in general, is that we always

write it off as whatever. And when mental health

issues aren't being addressed, they become repressed,

which causes the stress to rise even more!

We have to do a better job at handling each other a

little better!

Be a friend today.

Listen between the lines for the help our people are

asking for through their actions because they can't

formulate the words to express it verbally.

D.O.P.E. E.R.A.   Stanley Cox

Key Seven:
Respecting Others' Happiness

Message: Love, Happiness & Relationships

Sometimes the best way is to walk away. Save the

heartbreak.

Message: Love, Happiness & Relationships

Shout out to all the lovers. Just because you're lonely,

heartbroken, bitter, spiteful, angry or jealous don't be

a grouch and deny someone their happiness today!

HAPPY LOVE DAY!!!! Can't find someone to love or

love you back? LOVE YOURSELF!

D.O.P.E. E.R.A.   Stanley Cox

Message: Positivity Encouragement

There's nothing better than happiness. I HOPE ALL
OF YOU REACH A HIGH LEVEL OF HAPPINESS
IN YOUR LIFE. Try every day to reach that level and
if you can't do it for yourself, try and make someone
smile.

Message: Haterz

When you're on a winning streak you'll notice how
jealous, envious, sneaky, and hateful the ones you call
friends and family are.

That's why I Fuck with Em without Fucking with
EM!!!!!

Watch the ones that are close and make sure they do
what they're supposed to do.

D.O.P.E. E.R.A.   Stanley Cox

Message: Positivity & Encouragement

You ever had someone hit you and you ain't answer

for whatever reason, then they text you and say some

shit like, "I know you're up. I just saw you post..."

What?!?!

Are you really monitoring my page? Where they do

that at?

Ok so I posted something, that doesn't mean that I

feel like talking or texting. We all have our days

where we move at our own speed and there's

absolutely nothing wrong with that.

There are some days where you are forehead deep in

work only to come up for air once the task is

accomplished.

Go ahead and get your busy on.

D.O.P.E. E.R.A.   Stanley Cox

Go fill up your schedule, go get lost in your program.

At the end of the day, feel good about having

something to and never let anyone make you feel

different about handling your business!!!

RESPECT MY BUSY!!

Message: Positivity & Encouragement

Embrace new beginnings, especially if they're

positive.

Support your people who are transitioning as best

you can.

You would be shocked at how far a little

encouragement can go.

Message: Game

D.O.P.E. E.R.A.   Stanley Cox

Listen, the phrase: "I'm just saying," is hating!!

Stop being a damn critic unless you get paid to do

that, if not CLAP FOR A PERSON!!!

Be happy that a person is making themselves happy

doing what they're doing!!!!

Stop complaining, stop assuming, stop being messy

and noisy, stop wishing failure on people, stop

talking down about people and then upping yourself

in the same sentence.

NEGATIVITY IS WHACK!!

Love and light.

Message: Game

D.O.P.E. E.R.A.   Stanley Cox

STOP BEING AFRAID OF COMPETITION.

You are allowing your insecurities to get the best of

you!

Projecting your fears forms hatred in your mind and

fucks your thinking up!

We have to do better.

Remember it can get better if you work on it.

Message: Game

REMAIN PRICELESS, DON'T SELL OUT FOR

PENNIES!

Get up and get yourself in position.

Program your GPS towards the BAG!!!

It's always a game, you just gotta remember what

position you play and understand that making others

better is the test of a true leader and STAR.

D.O.P.E. E.R.A.   Stanley Cox

But you have to make sure you are ok first!

Message: Positivity & Encouragement

Peace of mind is established when sharing a piece of

mind. There are conversations that can iron out every

misunderstanding. Complications come when

people refuse to communicate.

Fault and responsibility dance to the same rhythm.

Some things may not be your fault, but you are still

responsible for them.

You wanna get the universe in your favor? Obey the

call of nature's dynamics.

People sometimes wonder how I remain so positive

in the midst of chaotic and catastrophic negativity

and I say the same thing time after time.

D.O.P.E. E.R.A.   Stanley Cox

Message: Positivity & Encouragement

I'm old enough to understand that some don't have

the understanding because some things can't be

understood from the angles people look at them.

If you change the way you look at things, the things

you look at begin to change.

I can only push this perspective on those who wish

to see light and I understand that dark minded

thinkers will have no interest in my vision.

I separate myself from anyone who wouldn't relight

my candle if they see it going out.

You have to surround yourself around the light.

It's the only way to stay LIT!!! (AYE)

Message: Positivity & Encouragement

D.O.P.E. E.R.A.   Stanley Cox

Know the nature of the beast you're dealing with and

never think for one second that you're completely

safe in the JUNGLE.

Even if you are looked at as a king.

Would you rather be the □ or the □?

When I was younger I wanted to be the lion.

As I get older, I have more aspirations to be like the

fox.

The fox is smart, a thinker, a planner, witty and

evasive.

Message: Positivity & Encouragement

Every day might not be a good day, but you can find

something good in every day.

D.O.P.E. E.R.A.   Stanley Cox

Message: Game

You have to wait your turn.

While you're waiting, be getting your game ready.

Get your mind right. Get your hustle on.

Study, research, work out, prepare, so when your

number is called,

You READY!!!!

Don't be so quick to win.

Don't run for class president just because you're

popular, if you're not ready to handle the

responsibilities that come with the position you're

running for.

Be blessed. Be smart.

Message: Game

D.O.P.E. E.R.A.   Stanley Cox

Know when you're the blessing you have to be the
bearer of other's burdens.

Message: Positivity & Encouragement

I find myself seeing the things in people no one else
can see. My visions make me go a little harder for
them. I've fought battles for individuals solely based
off hidden potential. I don't know if it was empathy
or sympathy, but I feel the need to take a little bit
more time with others.
I love my Brothers and Sisters, Friends and Family
passionately and I want the best for them. All I hope
is that they want the same for me.
But, you can't want something for someone more
than they want it for themselves

D.O.P.E. E.R.A.   Stanley Cox

We should focus on healing ourselves so that we can

be an example to our people that the healing process

is possible because LORD KNOWS WE NEED IT.

Message: Game

It's time we fix the leaks in our support systems.

Push mine like you'd push yours if you're really in

my corner!

Let me know that you're in my corner, not just in my

circle taking up space!

Message: Game

How enlightened can you be if you constantly throw

shade on others?

D.O.P.E. E.R.A.   Stanley Cox

If you are as enlightened as you proclaim to be, then

someone's happiness should make you happy even if

you're not responsible for it.

I don't care what you believe in, if you're happy and

it gives you hope and positive affirmation, then I'm

all for it.

Message: Game

Today you can resurrect yourself and rise from

behind the shadow of the clouds that have been

blocking your blessings.

Be the change that you wish to see!!

Smile, laugh, love and live.

D.O.P.E. E.R.A.   Stanley Cox

Message: Game

The cold thing about mental health in the hood or

the black community, in general, is that we always

write it off as whatever. And when mental health

issues aren't being addressed, they become repressed,

which causes the stress to rise even more!

We have to do a better job at handling each other a

little better!

Be a friend today.

Listen between the lines for the help our people are

asking for through their actions because they can't

formulate the words to express it verbally.

D.O.P.E. E.R.A.   Stanley Cox

Key Eight:
Giving Back

Message: Haterz

Strive to be better and refrain from becoming

BITTER!!

Message: Positivity Encouragement

The past will never change but we have the ability to

make the future whatever we want it to be. Don't be

ashamed of the past! Embrace it.

Message: Haterz

D.O.P.E. E.R.A.   Stanley Cox

Don't stunt on your folks, show them how to come

up. Encourage them, motivate them, support them

and never laugh at em!! Cause one thing about them

tables,

they ALWAYS TURN!!!!!!

Message: Goals, Hustle & Ambition

Protect dreams.

Encourage others.

And if you can, aid someone in following theirs,

especially if you are living yours.

Message: Goals, Hustle & Ambitions

Don't tell me dreams don't come true.

We're living proof.

D.O.P.E. E.R.A.   Stanley Cox

I stuck to the dream, focused, and didn't hold

grudges when they told me no.

I didn't wait when they hesitated on me and never

second guessed my individuality.

I walk on what I believe in!!!!!

Message: Goals, Hustle & Ambitions

This may not be much to anyone but the guys and I,

but we opened up a clothing store smack dead in the

middle of the hood. We're giving out jobs, giving out

opportunity, and getting many people who wouldn't

be in the same circle to be together.

It's about squashing beef, saving lives and giving

back.

D.O.P.E. E.R.A.   Stanley Cox

We're motivating dreamers and thinkers that it's

possible and pissing off the GENTRIFIERS. Keeping

Oakland OAKLAND!!!!!!

Message: Game

I have no problem allowing people to use me, but

when you misuse me or abuse my kindness, I get

agitated.

It can't always just be on me!!!!

Heavy is the head that wears the crown. Stop letting

your heart make the decisions in place of your head.

I love you, but I can't let empathy get the best of me!!!

Message: Positivity & Encouragement

We have to be held accountable at one point or

another.

D.O.P.E. E.R.A.   Stanley Cox

Let's support US and build each other up, providing

ladders and crutches for our people, only then can we

better develop our communities and societies.

We need to utilize our strength in numbers.

Stop crying and complaining to be accepted and start

living in harmony with our people.

Unfortunately, there are WEs that HATE us more

than THEY that hate us....

Think on that.

Message: Game

You must be mindful of your influence.

Any person in their right mind will never want to

consciously lead the members of their village down a

path that is actively destroying their tribe.

D.O.P.E. E.R.A.   Stanley Cox

Remember this, everyone gets old, but not everyone

GROWS UP....

Time to get your grown Man/Woman on people.

Let's rise above all the adversity and once we reach a

higher height, throw some ladders down for others to

climb up.

Message: Positivity & Encouragement

You can't be selfish with your blessings, as soon as

they come, share them.

The more blessings you put in the fire, the longer the

flame last.

Eternal flame comes from the energy you give back to

the universe.

Be legendary and secure your longevity.

Spread love!

D.O.P.E. E.R.A.   Stanley Cox

Key Nine:
Reinvent the Role
Model

Message: Positivity Encouragement

I know some real niggas who have never sold a drug

or shot a gun.

You don't have to be a street nigga to be real

#justbeyourself.

Some keep it 001. I like to keep it 100.

Be true to you and you'll last out here.

Message: Positivity & Encouragement

Don't just set the example, be the example!

If you lead, lead correctly.

D.O.P.E. E.R.A.   Stanley Cox

You can get bad karma for bad advisory.

Message: Game

We have to reinvent the role model if we wish to see

a change in the perspective of our society.

Message: Game

Children have no positive images to look up to. We

must paint positive images and be the examples we

wish to see in these streets!!!

It starts with opening up businesses and creating

employment, jobs, and inclusion.

WE ALL NEED SOMETHING TO BE A PART OF!!!!

D.O.P.E. E.R.A.   Stanley Cox

Message: Game

I am not the me you knew when you used to know

me.

My character has not weakened because I've

expanded my perspective.

My peace is far more protected.

Never let them keep you in a box.

When they speak on your caterpillar, show them

your butterfly.

Just never forget the process.

Message: Game

For several years we have glorified the Pimps, the

Drug dealers, the Killers, the Goons, the Robbers and

the Gangstas. We grew up idolizing those

D.O.P.E. E.R.A.   Stanley Cox

responsible for the destruction of our communities.

It is up to the new generation to rewrite their idols.

Reinvent the Role Models.

Look up to the Business owners, Lawyers, Judges,

Techies, College students, Teachers, Doctors,

Athletes and anyone else who gives hope and

inspiration.

Even if you're born in it, you don't have to stay in it.

We've endured the destruction of our communities

for several years, so overcoming the deficits won't

happen overnight, but we can start today!!!

Message: Game

Stop holding these entertainers and celebrities to

these impossible standards. They are human. They

D.O.P.E. E.R.A.   Stanley Cox

breathe the same oxygen you do and bleed the same

color.

Entertainers and Celebrities stop acting like you can

walk on water!

You're never too rich to be regular.

Dope Era Living.

Message: Goals, Hustle & Ambition

The big homie was the guy that didn't criticize you,

didn't judge you, and didn't jump to conclusions.

Instead, he taught you, helped you and healed you

when you were hurt.

They have removed the role of the big homie, so now

we have these youngsters who have raised

themselves and learned from trial and error while

being exploited by villains for not adhering to the

D.O.P.E. E.R.A.   Stanley Cox

rules and regulation of a street code that they know

nothing about.

Be a real big homie.

Let's reinvent the role model and stop being grown

ass kids.

Message: Positivity & Encouragement

Be unapologetically what you are.

I am unapologetically BLACK!

I'm Black and I'm proud. SAY IT LOUD!!!!

Message: Positivity & Encouragement

SUPPORT N.B.R.M. (New Black Role Models)

Reinvent the Role Model, change the mentality,

create new perspectives and more prosperous reality

shall follow.

D.O.P.E. E.R.A.   Stanley Cox

#DopeEraPhilosophy.

Message: Game

Brodies, if you're 35 and up, you have been selected as

a mentor.

In these streets, you have to be the "Big Homie".

You have to be a role model and lead the way for

these kids.

We gotta do better!!!!

Message: Love, Happiness & Relationships

Stop putting your babies in the arms of strangers and

then complain about them being mistreated.

Raise your babies.

Stop neglecting your dreams and go hard for your

children.

D.O.P.E. E.R.A.   Stanley Cox

I am focused on living for not only myself but my

kid's kids.

Message: Game

You're not my big homie, you're just older than me.

Stop promoting the deterioration of my critical

thinking through your manipulative influence.

THERE'S NO RIGHT WAY TO DO THE WRONG

THING.

You gonna build shit or bullshit?

You can see the bullshitters every day on your local

block.

They lie to the kids about their fabricated past,

glorifying all that NIGGA shit they've done.

I don't knock nobody or their hustle, but what I'm

not about to do is PROMOTE THE POISON THAT

HAS PLAGUED OUR PEOPLE.

D.O.P.E. E.R.A.   Stanley Cox

Message: Game

YOU GONNA BUILD SHIT OR BULLSHIT?

Life is about construction, not destruction.

Builders can never enjoy peace when they surround

themselves with destroyers.

The mind of a destroyer always drifts back into

destruction mode.

One will always resort to what they're comfortable

doing. When a boxer forgets what they trained for,

they get knocked out. Stick to your plan but remain

committed to change and excellence. One can't

approach life with the same perspective forever.

Things grow. If we are not growing, then we are

dead.

Don't kill your ability to grow!!!

#DopeEraPhilosophy.

D.O.P.E. E.R.A.   Stanley Cox

Message: Love, Happiness & Relationships

YOU ARE THE EMOTION YOU CARRY.

Create happiness and positive vibes.

BE BEAUTIFUL PEOPLE!!!

Spread love today.

Be thankful and appreciative for something and love

and shine bright light today.

#DopeEraEnergy.

Message: Game

Now if you've got 5 niggas that are disciplined,

determined, and dedicated, their blessings will be

abundant.

You can't roll with a pack of hyenas and expect the

rewards meant for lions.

D.O.P.E. E.R.A.   Stanley Cox

To be a King requires a lot of responsibility, sacrifice,

and seclusion.

Strength does not come from a physical muscle but

from a mental toughness.

You wanna just survive? Or survive and be

successful? BE GREAT!

Message: Game

Stop being afraid to give people credit.

Stop trying to trump people's accomplishments with

your past accolades.

Allow a person to deliver their acceptance speech,

learn to mute your anger and jealousy, and refrain

from giving your input when regarding matters that

don't determine whether you win or lose.

D.O.P.E. E.R.A.   Stanley Cox

As the old saying goes "what they eat don't make you shit," so why are you so interested in what's on their plate?

Stop being the "Mr. Me Too".

Stop being the "Ole I been Did That".

I made a promise to myself that I'd never be the old bitter rapper begging for attention.

You want your past relevancy to be talked about? It's easy,

REMAIN RELEVANT.

There's too much segregation in the world for someone to be mad about frivolous things.

Stay focused, take care of your family, know your friends, give back and most of all keep ascending.

And as you grow, never condemn people for things that you were once guilty of, especially if you're in a

D.O.P.E. E.R.A.   Stanley Cox

position to reach them and teach them and you defer

that option.

Message: Game

You're gonna have to live up to that role that you're

playing.

It's better to just be who you truly are at heart.

No fronting. No faking.

Everybody else is taken, so why try to be somebody

else?

Message: Positivity & Encouragement

I'm appreciative of my growth. I've seen what my

positive influence can bring forth.

We've done marvels in the community banning

together.

D.O.P.E. E.R.A.   Stanley Cox

Although some will never say it, they have studied
the blueprint we've laid out and reenacted similar
work (which is a great thing).
In my progressed perspective, I don't seek
acknowledgment.
I'm humbled that the work is being done.
Making a difference starts with yourself. Let's keep
building.
The real architects are those who cultivate the minds
of the forward thinkers, the youth!

Message: Positivity & Encouragement
You're a good player if you go out and put up 26
points, 9 rebounds, and 5 assists every night.
But if you make other players reach career highs
every night, you're a great player.

D.O.P.E. E.R.A.   Stanley Cox

Make them all stars (especially those who are

considered average).

Be the greatest you.

Message: Goals, Hustle Ambition

FUCK A TITLE. GET THAT CHECK!!!!!!

Stick to your set of principles

If you chose morals over money, you'll

always have respect.

But never look for approval from these

niggas.

There's too much jealousy and hatred!

#DopeEraorNoEra

D.O.P.E. E.R.A.   Stanley Cox

Message: Game

What's your put-up game like???? It's rare for a

person to get a million dollars at once (outside of

athletes, trust fund babies, and lucky lotto players).

Most people have invested time in their quest for

million(s). The average millionaire in America didn't

become a millionaire until their 40s.

Which means they have been stacking, investing and

flipping.

Unfortunately, my people in this generation cats

don't see themselves living that long, so they're in a

rush to bust. I love the phrase "A slow grind is better

than no grind" because with consistency and a good

hustle you'll have all that you desire in no time.

Find out what numbers work for you and get your

hustle on.

D.O.P.E. E.R.A.   Stanley Cox

Stop being in a rush to flash cash and show the world
how much you got.

I was taught that if you can count your money, then
your money doesn't count.

Ball in Private.

The fans will see your highlights. Stay focused and
work on your put-up game.

Stack and invest and distribute the extra amongst
your people. No weak links.

Message: Game

Niggas only care about themselves these days, so you
better just focus on doing the right thing.

Stay on the right side of right.

That's what it's about.

D.O.P.E. E.R.A.   Stanley Cox

Message: Game

Get it together lil homie. It ain't gon be easy, but

whatever comes quick, goes quicker.

Get some staying power. Be around for a minute

baby!!!

Message: Positivity & Encouragement

Never be happy about doing wrong.

There is no right way to do the wrong thing.

I received that message from my OG

@bop_bonafied one night and it stuck with

me.

BE MORE MINDFUL OF WHAT YOUR

PROUD OF.

D.O.P.E. E.R.A.   Stanley Cox

If you're doing wrong or had to do a little

wrong, let it be to get right!!

D.O.P.E. E.R.A.   Stanley Cox

Key 10:
Resilience, Accountability & Responsibility

Message: Goals, Hustle & Ambition

Stop confusing the hustle.

If you had to sin to get it, don't count it as a blessing

because you owe the GAME.

Message: Goals, Hustle & Ambition

Set a goal for today and go after it. Try your best to

accomplish it.

Remove yourself from all negative people and

opportunists.

D.O.P.E. E.R.A.   Stanley Cox

There's a thin line between hunger and hate.

Message: Goals, Hustle & Ambition

You lose it in the game, you get it back out of the

game.

Don't ever change positions or lose your identity

trying to climb out of a slump.

Stick to it. Stick to the plan.

Message: Goals, Hustle & Ambition

Strive to be somebody. Anyone can be nothing.

It's hella easy to do nothing.

Pick a goal and move forward.

Go after all your dreams and SOAR!!! #motivation

D.O.P.E. E.R.A.   Stanley Cox

Message: Game

GROW THRU WHAT YOU GO THRU. And then

wait until it's your turn at bat again.

Your time between bats should teach you more about

running bases in the batter box.

Message: Game

The difference between me & other people is that I

can admit my faults, own up to my bad decisions and

be open about them with no embarrassment.

I am never ashamed of anything I do or have done, say

or have said.

Are you?

D.O.P.E. E.R.A.   Stanley Cox

Message: Game

Don't allow your destiny to be determined by
another's success.

Get up & Get out and make your own way.

Fuck a handout. Be a standout on your own two
feet.

It's way better than sitting on all fours waiting on
these suckas with ego issues!!!

Motivation is better than MONEY

What's life without a positive ambition?

Message: Game

Don't forget you can be rich and still be broke!!!!

Never confuse knowing the price of something with
knowing the value of it.

D.O.P.E. E.R.A.   Stanley Cox

Sometimes we focus so much on who's hating that

we actually overlook the ones right underneath our

nose that are overflowing with love....

BE GREAT TODAY!

Message:Game

We can't control the hands we are dealt but we have

to understand that all cards aren't meant to be played

at once.

BE SMART THE DECK IS SHORT.

Be selective in how and who you expose your hand

to.

One card at a time, baby!!!!

D.O.P.E. E.R.A.   Stanley Cox

Message: Haterz

Stop falsely blaming others for your own downfall.

Take responsibility and be held accountable for the

bad choices you've made or make.

Let's build not destroy.

Message: Positivity & Encouragement

Don't worry about being slept on. They will review

what they have overlooked.

Keep working while they sleep and when they wake

up you'll be far ahead.

First, they act like they don't see you, but then they

copy your whole blueprint like they wanna be you!!!

They leave you to fend for yourself until they need

you!!!!!

Message: Positivity & Encouragement

D.O.P.E. E.R.A.   Stanley Cox

STOP COMPARING your accomplishments to

others' achievements.

If you're in the game for the long run, why are you

worried about the score in the first quarter????

Keep your head in the game and keep playing to the

best of your ability and all will pan out just right!!!

Message: Goals, Hustle & Ambition

Don't tell me it's not possible to achieve what you

want. Can't no dope fiends in the hood ever say that

I sold them crack, can't no young nigga ever say I told

him wrong.

THIS WAS ALL MY GRIND.

PEN AND PAD....

D.O.P.E. E.R.A.   Stanley Cox

It might take a little longer because I didn't sell my

soul or take no penitentiary chances to get it, but it

will come!!!

LOVE LIFE AND DON'T LET NO HATING STOP

YOU FROM LETTING YOUR LIGHT SHINE!!!!

Message: Haterz

Stop falling for the bait.

We live in a time where people will say anything for

a reaction.

Once you give it to em, that's their VICTORY.

KINGS AND QUEENS, SIT BACK AND OBSERVE

THE MOVES OF THE PAWNS.

They can't even approach us without permission!!!

STOP GIVING THEM ACCESS.

D.O.P.E. E.R.A.   Stanley Cox

Message: Game

You have to be present when your blessing is to be

delivered.

Keep getting in position. You gotta be available.

Grind for it, don't whine for it.

Message: Positivity & Encouragement

Never be just your possessions because once they're

lost, they lose respect for you!!!!

Stay consistent and stay grinding.

Holding grudges will only hold you back!!!!!

#DopeQuotes

Message: Goals, Hustle & Ambition

D.O.P.E. E.R.A.   Stanley Cox

The truth doesn't go as far as the lies!!!!!!!

Stand on your truth no matter what!

But, always know that people will try their best to

turn your name through the dirt.

Only you become the fool when you try to prove

them wrong.

We are living in a world where if you're the only one

keeping it real you seem fake and if enough people

say the same fake shit about you without facts, proof

or truth, the followers of the world run with it. By

the time the real truth comes out, your name has

already been dragged through the mud and the

people who can clean it don't like you or have already

said that fuck shit about you, so they can't keep it ☐

cause they don't wanna seem fake to they peers.

So, the bullshit continues!!

D.O.P.E. E.R.A.   Stanley Cox

Let's end the ignorance and push real life.

I forgive all the dirt throwers because my truth is

rooted in solid principles.

Stay focused out here!!!

Message: Positivity & Encouragement

Never compromise your peace for profit.

Embrace happiness beyond material possessions.

If money is all you have, you don't have much!!!!!

Remember that there's a lot of RICH PEOPLE WITH

POOR SOULS

Message: Positivity & Encouragement

I was never perfect.

I never had it all. I didn't come from rich parents. My

Mother, a hard-working hustler, was on her own at

D.O.P.E. E.R.A.   Stanley Cox

13 because she refused to live in a house with 10 other

sisters and brothers.

So, she hit the streets hustling to survive, running

with Ballers, Gangstas, Pimps, and the Gurus of the

underworld.

My Father, the baby of 4, was a smooth criminal, a

con artist, a crook, a hustler, a pimp and a junkie.

But, he was a man who loved me unconditionally.

I got it Honest early.....my Father and Mother died.

It's been a long road for me, but I'm still in the

beginning stages of the highway. I'm thankful and

humbled by all the mishaps in life.

I stay happy when I could be directed down a road of

anger, and frustration.

I woke up this morning fully thankful and rejoiced.

I told all my folks how proud I am of them.

D.O.P.E. E.R.A.   Stanley Cox

BLACK MEN CAN MAKE IT FROM ACTIVITIES

THAT DON'T INVOLVE SELLIN DRUGS,

TAKING, HATING, ETC.!!!!!!

Be great Black Man. Be great Black Sister.

There is beauty in all creations.

Spread love the world is full of too much

hate!!!!!!!!!!!!!!!!!!!!!!!!!

Message: Goals, Hustle & Ambition

Sometimes the things you see, everyone else is blind

to.

I've pondered allowing my mind to wander far

beyond realities grasp.

I'm lost in my imagination but am willing to bring

this fantasy to fruition.

D.O.P.E. E.R.A.   Stanley Cox

Maybe I am the only one who sees it, but like the sweater says "One day it will all make sense .....(and cents)"

Message: Game

One's character shouldn't be judged or valued by their possessions. The true testament of one's character comes from one's response to adversity.
Adversity gives definition to structure.
It's easy to drive a smooth road with a roadmap, a straight highway with fresh pavement.
But to be able to navigate a winding road with torn and ravaged pavement, potholes, speed bumps, no lights and no GPS and still be able to get to your destination is a true sign of a journeyman accepting the challenge of their adventure.

D.O.P.E. E.R.A.   Stanley Cox

No one said it would be easy.

SEE IT THRU!!!!

Message: Game

You are what you entertain. If you are constantly

engrossed in the comment section, you allow your

mind and attention span to be consumed with the

pettiness. I've endured several tumultuous situations

in my life. But I realize that nothing has broken me

to a point that is beyond return. Now I'll admit that

I've felt like giving up. I've cried, I've vented, I've

prayed, I've meditated, and I've lashed out.

But most importantly, I've gathered myself and put

the pieces back together. Anybody in this life that

tries to appear perfect has insecurities that they're

hiding. My life has always been an open book an I've

D.O.P.E. E.R.A.   Stanley Cox

invited the world to read it. My mistakes have

shaped my perspective and my mishaps have added

flavor to my character. Adversity has molded my

motivation and loses have taught me lessons.

My lowest moments gave me high expectations.

I'm human, a regular guy living his dream and

showing the world that it won't always go your way,

nor will it go away. But keep pushing because in the

end it will be ok, and if it's not ok then it's not the

end.

Message: Positivity & Encouragement

There are many obstacles that we all face in life. The

true definition of a person's character is not what he

does when everything is going well but how he

responds when things have gone bad. I've suffered

D.O.P.E. E.R.A.   Stanley Cox

through too many things in my life to allow small

obstacles to stop my objective. My main objective is

to continue to inspire people to aspire to be whatever

it is that they wish to be.

No one escapes life alive.

On this journey, there will be many roadblocks, but

you have to realize that there's more than one way to

the top.

Don't just look for one path, stay focused, stay

driven, and continue to drive through all climates.

Some days it's going to rain, some days it's going to

snow, some days it's going to be pretty.

Stop counting the days. Make the days count.

When you think you are having a bad day, try

missing one.

D.O.P.E. E.R.A.   Stanley Cox

Message: Goals, Hustle & Ambition

I refuse to wait on a man for a handout or ask

someone to do something for me that I can do myself.

It's just funny to me that a man would complain

about what you did or didn't do for him when he had

the opportunity to do it for himself.

No pride. No ego.

I've never been afraid to ask for help, but if the help

or assistance doesn't come I won't still be sitting

there like I can't do it without them. It might take a

little longer without help but I can endure the

struggle, I'm from Oakland.

That's a struggle in itself and a success story to even

still be here!!!!!

My Era was Dope...and I am still Dope.

D.O.P.E. E.R.A.   Stanley Cox

Message: Goals, Hustle & Ambition

Don't allow another man to control your destiny.

No man should have that much power over you.

I might not have it now, but I promise, with my

focus, ambition, drive, and talent, I'll get it.

Up until then, Ima be thuggin behind them project

buildings!

GRIND FOR IT, DON'T WHINE FOR IT!

The Era was Dope, taught me how to hustle.

Message: Positivity & Encouragement

Sisters, don't get so caught up in trying to make a

man discover his worth that you sacrifice your value!

Don't let bad love dim your light!!!!

D.O.P.E. E.R.A.   Stanley Cox

You tell yourself all the time that you can't live

without them, but what kind of life is it trying to

keep somebody that don't wanna be kept!!!!

Either accept the fact he will be what he is or walk

away.

Anything other than that will risk your life or liberty.

Message: Game

Never hurt a snake.... KILL IT.

Never supply more rope to the people you have cut

off.

D.O.P.E. E.R.A.   Stanley Cox

Once you realize their selfishness, avoid them

because it can possibly come back and hurt you.

The same people that expect you to run laps won't

even speed walk for you!!!!

Message: Positivity & Encouragement

We must unlearn the things that we were taught to

us by people who didn't know. We must not be

cursed by the ignorance and lack of knowledge of

people who for generations and generations have

been trained to compete in a fools Olympics.

One must rewrite the papers.

Message: Haterz

D.O.P.E. E.R.A.   Stanley Cox

Why would you want a friend, a peer, or a colleague

of yours to compromise their peace and blessings for

your burdens????

People get involved in things personally and then

they want everyone they know to fight their battles.

Then they have the audacity to be mad at someone

who doesn't do it

Be careful of the treacherous ones in your circles.

#DopeEraObstacles.

Message: Game

Stop confusing friendships.

Some people just know you.

It doesn't mean y'all cool.

There's a big difference between ASSOCIATES AND

FRIENDS.

D.O.P.E. E.R.A.   Stanley Cox

Don't be FOOLED.

Save yourself the heartache and heartbreak and

know the situation you're in.

You can't change who some people are.

Message: Positivity & Encouragement

Our mind has always been the most precious jewel

and our contribution to this universe.

Remember we built pyramids before we inhabited

projects.

Deteriorate the mind and the unfolding of the people

shall follow.

Strengthen the mind and Gods greatest creation

appears "A PROGRESSED PERSPECTIVE."

You change your perception and you change your

reality.

D.O.P.E. E.R.A.   Stanley Cox

Life is not about what you're looking at, but what

you see.

Speak your mind, seek understanding and search for

signs of growth.

What isn't growing is dead.

Message: Positivity & Encouragement

All organisms grow.

Change is a necessity.

As you progress, you pay homage to life's lessons.

Grow through what you go through.

Make yourself available for the blessings. I used to

crack jokes with the old heads like, "Man, you Niggas

hella old. Get yo ass outta here".

And an old man once told me, "You gotta live to get

old. I've earned these gray hairs. Pray you get some...."

D.O.P.E. E.R.A.   Stanley Cox

PERSPECTIVE.

Message: Goals, Hustle & Ambition

Ask yourself what has complaining improved for

you?

Do you feel better after you hate on someone?

How does it make you feel to know all the time you

spend worrying about what someone else is doing

doesn't slow their progress, it only distracts you from

your projects?

I don't care what anyone else is doing,.

The only time I put my concern on the line is when

I'm motivated by others.

Make allies and associates, not enemies and

adversaries

D.O.P.E. E.R.A.   Stanley Cox

Message: Goals, Hustle & Ambition

One is never above the rules of the world, although

you may feel elevated due to your success. There are

rules that we all must abide by.

No one is exempt from the game, so it's the small

things that we must be mindful of. Some things as

simple as locking the door behind you, keeping your

valuables safe, protecting your peace and never

allowing the dollar to dominate your demeanor.

It hurts when things are lost, stolen, taken, or

displaced.

We search for reasons and excuses and people to

blame for them.

But the majority of the time, we only have ourselves

to blame.

D.O.P.E. E.R.A.   Stanley Cox

No matter how devastating the loss may be, if it's

self-inflicted then TAKE IT ON THE CHIN!

The game will replace it.

Stay focused, pay attention to the small details and

most of all, BE RESPONSIBLE.

Message: Haterz

You build shit or bullshit.

Pick now. Today is the first day of the future you.

Be great.

Take all the knives that people have thrown at you

and carve out a piece of this pie!!!

Take all the bricks they throw at you and build you a

foundation.

Take the hate they throw at you and build a love

machine.

D.O.P.E. E.R.A.   Stanley Cox

Whatever you do, don't let this shit break you!!!

#DopeEraMotivation.

Message: Game

Appreciate your blessings and learn from your

lessons.

Don't let anything knock your hustle!!!

They would love to see you stop so they can brag

about being responsible for it.

You're gonna need to do a little more.

This is a divine mission.

I promised my mother and daughter I wasn't

quitting!!!

Message: Game

D.O.P.E. E.R.A.   Stanley Cox

A person's true character can only be shown when adversity is staring them in the face, breathing down their neck, and pushing them against the wall.

You gonna hold or fold?

I made a vow to my mother and myself that I ain't letting nothing stop me.

Only death will be able to take me away from pursuing my dreams and goals and representing what I bring to the table.

Message: Game

Keep people in your circle that wanna add value to it, even when they not directly involved.

Love is light. Keep those around you that wanna see you glow!!!!!

D.O.P.E. E.R.A.   Stanley Cox

Message: Game

We have to be more mindful of those we call friends

in addition to being mindful of the jungle that we

dwell in.   .

The security in safe surroundings is a lesson one

must value far beyond any earthly possession

(especially if you wish to keep your possessions).

Message: Game

Perception is personal.

As long as have your rules and regulations in order

who's to say what's right or wrong for you...Just

D.O.P.E. E.R.A.   Stanley Cox

remember there is no right way to do the wrong

thing!!!!

#DopeEraPerspective.

Message: Game

It's not about how far you go in life it's about how far

you've come.

Some people at the top but the top wasn't but a few

steps away meanwhile others made it to level 3 but

they started at negative 9.

I respect the journey of any traveling man and those

who respect those who don't have.

If you've ever been a have not and you get a chance to

have lots, respect the VOYAGE.

Don't brag. Just be proud gracefully!!

D.O.P.E. E.R.A.   Stanley Cox

I'm thankful for everything and humbled by what's to

come!!!!

Blessings and lessons.

Message: Positivity & Encouragement

What yo bounce-back game like?

Everybody falls in life, but it's personal decision to

stay down.

No matter what I'm faced with, I'll face it.

If you can't deal with something sober, then you're

not really facing it because you're masking it.

Message: Positivity & Encouragement

Let's focus on the love.

Love is the foundation.

D.O.P.E. E.R.A.   Stanley Cox

The temple of Knowledge starts with the love of life
and the desire to show the light to others.

#sundaysermon

Message: Game

Nobody is at fault but yourself when it comes to the
repercussions of things you agreed to.
You can't sign a contract then say somebody fucked
you over because you didn't read the fine print.
You can't create a situation then complain about the
results when it gets out of control.
Hold yourself accountable and be responsible for
your decision-making!

Message: Game

D.O.P.E. E.R.A.   Stanley Cox

It is imperative that you treat everyone with love and respect regardless of their title or position. My granny would always say "you never too up to be down", so don't walk around like that hot air balloon can't be deflated.

Don't shun people because their appearance appears to be lower than yours.

You never know when you're entertaining an Angel.

You're never too rich to have common courtesy, never too beautiful for a hello or a hi.

The richest people in this world spiritually broke because they're piss poor morally.

Be blessed.

Always stay rich in spirit, with one billion dollars or one dollar.

That could be you.

D.O.P.E. E.R.A.   Stanley Cox

We are all only one mistake away from sleeping in a

park.

Today's janitor could be tomorrow's CEO.

D.O.P.E. E.R.A.   Stanley Cox

Conclusion

Still blind to a broken man's dream? Still trying to figure out
how that rose grew from the concrete? You still will rather
discuss the how while ignoring the why. How about you
acknowledge the pedals from that rose, enjoy its story, this
same rose that grew with no water, no light, only sun-rays it
experienced was when the sun played peek a boo thru the cracks
of the projects, but it still rose

"STILL I RISE" like in the words of two of the greatest writers
the 20th century was blessed to have. DR. Maya Angelou and
Professor Tupac Shakur.

As you get older perception plays a major role in your life's
choices, because you begin to pay more attention to detail, and
knowledge blesses you with insight. Growth allows the
application of understanding to process that's it's no longer
what you're looking at, but more so what you see.

Sight & Vision are two different things. But it's takes wisdom
to understand the difference. Sight is and ability to see what's
visible, vision is the knowledge and intelligence to know it's
always more than what you see.

D.O.P.E. E.R.A.   Stanley Cox

Overlooked are priceless gems hidden in the beds of rubble confused for debris.

What I wish for you that's reading this right now, the objective is not for you to take on my train of thought but for you to recognize the importance of staying focused and being able to prevent the derailing of your Train. Leave no confusion in my conclusion

The sole purpose of this book was to relight the lamp of guidance that my generation has seemed to purposefully stop utilizing.

To be a voice of reason to the misguided youth, at the same time creating a course that avoids collision.

A vast majority of children from my generations grew up without Fathers, forcing them to fend for themselves, so much that they became detached from reliance developing a disdaining attitude towards Authority. So, anyone trying to be "Fathers" or authoritative Like figures they expeditiously disregard them.

Knowing what I'm up against I don't set out to be anyone other than LIBBY's Daddy. But I do wish to reinvent the Role model and become the big homie I wish I had growing up.

D.O.P.E. E.R.A.   Stanley Cox

not the one who manipulates the youth but the one that motivates them. If you believe than you can achieve I mean HELL just look at me...

Pac said that he wouldn't be the one that changes the world, but he would spark the mind of the person who does. Rather I change the world or not thru my work I hope to alter the perception of many of my constituents who can't see pass their boxed in paradigm.

They often tell me "Fabby you should run for Mayor" .... not in a million years did I have that on my to do list growing up but hey you never know I'm just keeping a positive perspective, staying Dope, glad I'm able to receive my roses while I can appreciate the smell.

So much negativity in this world I'm just pushing peace to my people, respecting others happiness as I would hope they'd respect mine. Since I'm my own biggest Fan regardless if the world likes this book or not just to say I'm a published author I'm super excited......" Momma I WROTE BOOK"

Lil bad ass Stanley with A.D.H.D sat down and really Penned a book Hahahaha!

I'm giving back because if you know then you owe. It's all a part of resilience, responsibility and accountability being a father and a public figure but always pushing fatherhood over the figures

D.O.P.E. E.R.A.   Stanley Cox

In the END it will be ok and if it's not ok

Then it's not the END.......

I'm to anointed to be disappointed

So, I'll leave the same way I came

In peace in harmony

*Hoping the supreme being maybe pleased with my
contributions to this realm...*

*Big thank you to all of the supporters along the journey this is
just the first of many ....*

The era way

D.O.P.E. E.R.A.   Stanley Cox

D.O.P.E. E.R.A.   Stanley Cox

D.O.P.E. E.R.A.   Stanley Cox

D.O.P.E. E.R.A.   Stanley Cox

D.O.P.E. E.R.A.   Stanley Cox

D.O.P.E. E.R.A.   Stanley Cox

D.O.P.E. E.R.A.   Stanley Cox

D.O.P.E. E.R.A.   Stanley Cox